CREDENTIALS FOR GENEALOGISTS

PROOF OF THE PROFESSIONAL

Paul Gorry

GORRY RESEARCH

BALTINGLASS, IRELAND.

Gorry Research
84 Ardglass, Baltinglass, Co. Wicklow, W91RH59, Ireland

www.gorryresearch.ie

Published in Ireland in 2018

British Library Cataloguing in Publication Data
ISBN 978-1-9164480-0-1

Typeset and printed in Ireland.

In memory of my generous &
knowledgeable mentors,

Eileen O'Byrne, FAGI

(1922-2016)

&

Eilish Ellis, FAPGI

(1919-2009)

Acknowledgements

In acknowledging help with this book I take the opportunity to thank those who set me on the path in a hobby-profession that has been a wonderful experience. Kathleen McDermott, my inspirational aunt, was the first person to encourage my fascination with the past and to feed my hunger for knowledge of my unknown ancestors. That journey began when I was about seven years old. In my teens another aunt, Marjorie Gorry, provided family history information she eked out for me, and brought me on my first archaeological society excursion. At the Genealogical Office, where I joined the freelance research panel at the age of nineteen, I received friendship, guidance and encouragement from Eileen O'Byrne, Eilish Ellis and Alita Dûsek. These people set me on the road to a lifetime in genealogical research.

For help in preparing this book, firstly, I wish to thank the twenty professional genealogists of standing who responded to my questionnaire. They cannot be named here because, when asking for honest and forthright answers, I promised them anonymity. However, I can say that they included ten practitioners without credentials and ten with credentials, and that they were from various locations spread across North America, the British Isles, Continental Europe and Australasia.

Secondly, I wish to thank to following genealogists for their guidance and information, in some cases proofreading and correcting relevant parts of the text: Andrea Bentschneider, Chairwoman of *Verband deutschsprachiger Berufsgenealogen;* Janet Bishop, FSGRA; Anthony J. Camp, MBE, FGRA; Laurence Harris, genealogist specialising in Jewish ancestry; Jennifer Harrison, historian & genealogist; Alan Jakman, editor of *More Maiorum*; Sue McBeth, MAAGRA; Alan MacLeod, President of ASGRA; Allan Marble, CG(C); Ian Marson, FGRA; Robert Pierce, CG(C); Dianne Snowden, AM, MAAGRA; Pierre Soucy, *directeur général de la Fédération québécoise des sociétés de généalogie;* Geoff Swinfield, AGRA; Anne Young, MAAGRA; and Faye Young, MAAGRA.

I owe an enormous debt to my friends Cora Crampton, Mihail Evans, Orla O'Sullivan and Steven Smyrl, MAGI, for proofreading the text of this book, correcting errors, suggesting improvements and advising entire rearrangements. Their generous help was invaluable. My thanks also to Simone Hassett-Costello who is responsible for the lay out of this book and the cover design.

I also wish to thank my young artist friend, Dion Bajrami, for his variations on 'The Man' which are scattered through the book. This figure is based on the symbol of St Matthew from the Book of Durrow. A tree of 'The Man' figures is the emblem I adopted for Gorry Research decades ago. My earliest known Gorry ancestors were buried in Durrow and Matthew was a name used in several generations of the family.

Finally, I must acknowledge that readers will discern a leaning towards Ireland and Irish genealogical matters in the text. This betrays my greater intimacy with things Irish, which could not be ignored, and for which I apologise.

Abbreviations

ACCREDITING ORGANISATIONS

AAGRA	Australasian Association of Genealogists and Record Agents
AGI	Accredited Genealogists Ireland
AGRA	Association of Genealogists and Researchers in Archives
ASGRA	Association of Scottish Genealogists and Researchers in Archives
BCG	Board for Certification of Genealogists
BQACG	Bureau québécois d'attestation de compétence en généalogie
CAFG	Council for the Advancement of Forensic Genealogy
GIM	Genealogical Institute of the Maritimes
ICAPGen	International Commission for the Accreditation of Professional Genealogists

PROFESSIONAL CREDENTIALS

AG	Accredited Genealogist
AGRA	Member of the Association of Genealogists and Researchers in Archives
AGRA Associate	Associate of the Association of Genealogists and Researchers in Archives
ASGRA	Member of the Association of Scottish Genealogists and Researchers in Archives

Associate of AGRA	Associate of the Association of Genealogists and Researchers in Archives
CG	Certified Genealogist
CG(C)	Certified Genealogist [Canada]
CGL	Certified Genealogical Lecturer
FAGI	Fellow of Accredited Genealogists Ireland
FCG	ForensicGenealogistCredentialed
FGRA	Fellow of the Association of Genealogists and Researchers in Archives
FSGRA	Fellow of the Association of Scottish Genealogists and Researchers in Archives
GFA	Généalogiste de filiation agréé / Certified Lineage Genealogist
GRA	Généalogiste recherchiste agréé / Certified Genealogical Researcher
GRS(C)	Genealogical Record Searcher [Canada]
MAAGRA	Member of the Australasian Association of Genealogists and Record Agents
MAGI	Member of Accredited Genealogists Ireland
MGA	Maître généalogiste agréé / Certified Master Genealogist

SUPPORT / NETWORKING ORGANISATIONS / PROFESSIONAL CHAMBERS

APG	Association of Professional Genealogists
APH	Association of Personal Historians
BALH	British Association for Local History
CEGS	Compagnie Européenne des Généalogistes Successoraux
CGP	Chambre des Généalogistes Professionnels
CGSF	Chambre des Généalogistes Successoraux de France
CIGP	Chambre Internationale des Généalogistes Professionnels
CSGF	Chambre Syndicale des Généalogistes de France
FPAR	Federation of Probate and Asset Researchers
GSG	Genealogical Speakers Guild

IOHA	International Oral History Association
ISFHWE	International Society of Family History Writers and Editors
ISOGG	International Society of Genetic Genealogy
SYGENE	l'Alliance des généalogistes professionnels

OTHER RELEVANT ABBREVIATIONS

ASG	American Society of Genealogists
CPD	Continuing Professional Development
DipFHS	Diploma in Family Historical Studies
FQSG	Fédération québécoise des sociétés de généalogie
Gen-Fed	Genealogical Institute on Federal Records
GPS	Genealogical Proof Standard
GSU	Genealogical Society of Utah
IHGS	Institute of Heraldic and Genealogical Studies
LDS	Church of Jesus Christ of Latter-day Saints
PLCGS	Professional Learning Certificate in Genealogical Studies
RQG	Register of Qualified Genealogists
SAG	Society of Australian Genealogists
SoG	Society of Genealogists
UGA	Utah Genealogical Association

x

Contents

Preface

Professional credentials have been available for professional genealogists in some parts of the world for over half a century. The primary reasons for introducing them were to protect both practising genealogists and their clients from the ever-present dangers of rogue or incompetent researchers who were tarnishing the reputation of the profession. Credentials were introduced to guarantee integrity, competence and experience.

There are more people throughout the world today than ever before calling themselves professional genealogists. Most of them do not have professional credentials. Some do not see any reason to seek them because they have a good personal reputation. Some feel that taking a higher educational course is a substitute for credentials. Some are possibly intimidated by the criteria for accreditation. Some do not have the option to obtain credentials because of geographical or linguistic barriers. Others, unfortunately, have no intention of ever testing themselves against any standards because they know the inevitable outcome.

Potential clients seeking a professional genealogist may be misled by the information that the individual is a member of this-or-that organisation with an impressive-sounding name. Most will not realise that membership of such organisations involves nothing more than paying an annual fee. Some are general membership societies for anyone with an interest in researching a particular area or ethnic group. Others are support or networking organisations for practitioners. None of these test the competence and experience of those they admit to membership.

However, there are several long-established, internationally known organisations that offer accreditation to professional genealogists. They are not elitist or limiting, but rather *enabling*. They have different criteria and methods of assessment, but they all test the competence and experience of applicants before they provide them with credentials.

Educational courses are becoming more and more popular as an introduction to the profession. It is important to remember that they are not the only route to developing a career in genealogy. How one gains competence and experience should not matter when it comes to gaining a credential. Unfortunately, there is a relatively new element within genealogy that seeks to replace professional credentials with academic barriers. This does a great disservice to genealogy and to hundreds of passionate family historians who wish to turn their acquired knowledge and experience into a career.

I hope this book will convince readers that professional credentials are the best way to protect clients while providing an avenue to a career in research for the true genealogist.

Introduction

Ancestral research has been a passion for me for as long as I can remember, and I have worked in it professionally since the age of nineteen. It was from concern for the future and the integrity of genealogy as a profession that I decided to write this book. I believe that credentials are important for the protection of practitioners and their clients. Please remember this as you read, if you read, because in championing the cause of accreditation I may say things that are unpalatable even for the organisations that provide credentials.

Genealogy currently is in a state of flux. Things are changing at such a rate that there is a general lack of direction. Commercial data providers are so busy competing for their share of a growing market that they must constantly come up with new material to attract subscribers to their websites. At the same time the giant data providers are squeezing out smaller ones or buying up their assets. Record repositories are finding it increasingly difficult to get family historians across the threshold because so many of their holdings are now on their websites, or commercial ones. Long-established family history societies are struggling to attract new members. Conferences are becoming redundant, unless they morph into trade fairs or wave DNA testing and technology in people's faces. And then there is the phenomenal population explosion among 'professional genealogists', disproportionate to the number of genealogists holding credentials.

Those new to tracing their family history are seduced by advertising and made to think that they must subscribe to this-or-that website: that using a database will lead them back in time with relative ease, just as happens to celebrities on television. They assume that everything in every record repository is now online, or should be. People more canny about the whole process often come to the realisation that they could do with professional help, whether it be a consultation or commissioned search. So, where does one find a professional genealogist?

There is nothing hard about finding any number of people purporting to be professional genealogists. They are everywhere to be seen. One organisation claims to represent nearly 2,800 such individuals worldwide. The Internet is crammed with impressive looking websites and blogs by people exuding expertise and professionalism. They are members of various organisations. They have visited all kinds of record repositories, have attended all sorts of events or courses and have all types of qualifications. How does a client choose from amongst all these experts?

I am a medical doctor. I am a lawyer.
I am a professional genealogist.
None of these statements are true, but only two will send me to jail. The first two professions require an individual to meet minimum standards before being permitted to hang out a shingle. Anyone can claim to be a professional genealogist. This demonstrates the problem that exists in trying to evaluate someone to hire as a genealogist.

- Gary Mokotoff, 'Hiring a Professional Genealogist: A Client's View', Avotaynu, Vol. IX, No. 2 (1993)

As someone who has been working in this area for nearly forty years, I believe that there are five important hallmarks to look for in a professional genealogist: (1) ETHICS, (2) KNOWLEDGE, (3) SKILL, (4) EXPERIENCE and (5) PROFESSIONAL CREDENTIALS. Nearly everyone setting out their stall as a professional genealogist will loudly proclaim that they subscribe to some code of ethics or other. This is good. It means that they promise not to take your money and run. Whether they have the knowledge, skill and experience to match their honesty needs more investigation. There are many practitioners out there who have the first four hallmarks, without ever seeking the fifth. These are very reputable individuals. There are ways that you might try to identify them but, if you want to be sure of a genealogist's abilities without the bother of researching their suitability, look for someone who has credentials. Not only should a professional with credentials be honest, knowledgeable, skilled and experienced, but if their work falls short of your expectations you have an organisation from which to seek redress.

Beginning in the 1960s in the USA and in the United Kingdom, a great amount of thought and effort went into developing professional credentials in various parts of the world. With people of questionable ability advertising their services as genealogists, these organisations were set up to provide a guarantee of competence to potential clients, and to provide a credential to genuine professionals. This is why today we have accrediting organisations in the USA, Canada, the British Isles and Australasia.

I have known some genealogists, like myself, whose passion for family history was ignited in childhood and who found their way at an early age into a career in genealogy. Most people who end up working as professional genealogists have had a lifetime of experience in another career. For some, an obsession with genealogy remained an amateur pursuit, while they got on with raising a family or working at something more lucrative that paid the bills until they took early retirement. For others, genealogy was a bug that only infected them later in life. Yet others saw genealogy from the outside as an expanding field and entered it for purely pragmatic business reasons.

People who have had another career before becoming professional genealogists often bring something extra to their approach to ancestral research. I have known people who, in a former life, were housewives, research scientists, accountants, dancers, barristers, music teachers, archaeologists, civil servants, draftsmen, science teachers, university lecturers, nurses, policemen, art teachers, technologists, hotel managers and textile designers.

What they all had in common was the genealogy-bug, along with knowledge and skill acquired over years of experience. They each took their own route to acquiring that knowledge and skill, whether by trial and error, joining a family history society, serving an informal apprenticeship, attending a course, or a combination of all these and more. One of the great things about genealogy (and, by extension, professional genealogy) is that there are many routes to learning its twists and turns.

If there is anything that the modern world has taught us it is that children learn at different speeds and in different ways: so too do adults. We often hear of very brilliant or successful people – Vincent Van Gogh, Winston Churchill, Mary Berry, Richard Branson, Whoopi Goldberg, Ryan Gosling – who were unhappy at school or hated the system or underachieved in exams, and who only gained in confidence when they found their niche. Adults who have pursued a variety of different careers meet in genealogical research on a level playing field. Here they can learn at their own speed and in their own way. If they acquire knowledge and skill and gain experience, and then wish to pursue professional research, there is no person or organisation telling them that their way is barred. If they are good enough at the work they can apply for accreditation and gain it.

But genealogy is in a state of flux. On one hand we have returned to the free-for-all days before professional credentials, with far more people purporting to be professional genealogists than there are individuals with credentials. On the other hand we have promoters of academic courses wishing to limit access to the profession to those who have gained the 'qualifications' in genealogy designed by them. Both extremes undermine the work of the accrediting organisations established to protect genuine professional genealogists and their clients.

It has to be said that the reason why many genuine professional genealogists may disregard credentials may be attributable in part to the accrediting organisations themselves. Having looked into the criteria, the application processes and the duration of credentials operated by the various bodies, I can see why in some cases they may be downright unattractive or even frightening to anyone trying to make a living as a genealogist. There is a delicate balance between convincing the wider world that you have stringent professional standards and convincing potential applicants that these standards are achievable or even worth seeking.

Another criticism that may be laid at the door of some of the accrediting bodies is that they do little or no promotion. If the general public is unaware of an organisation's existence the organisation is not doing a lot for the genealogists it is accrediting. I realise that the problem in most cases is that the organisation is small and run by volunteers, but promotion is vital and not necessarily expensive, and those accredited by the organisation should be encouraged to help promote it.

For all their possible shortcomings, accrediting bodies are not solely responsible for the return to the free-for-all days. A large part of the blame may be rightly placed at the door of networking bodies. These organisations have a major role to play in professional genealogy in terms of sharing information and ideas, and putting professionals in touch with one another. It is when they turn their attention to the public and promote their members' skills that they are in danger of usurping the role of accrediting organisations.

In some cases it is their name that is misleading to the public: in some cases it is their heavy promotion without full disclosure of the nature of the organisation and its limitations. The general public sees the name of an organisation for professional genealogists, sees a promotional symbol, sees that it fosters professionalism and that its members have a code of practice. The general public may be excused for thinking that this is an accrediting body.

If you were looking to fast-track a career in genealogy would you spend a few years building up your skills and preparing an application for an accrediting body, or would you pay a fee to a networking organisation to get instant access to a market? Some networking organisations can become a haven for people with little or no genealogical skills or experience. Such people can hide among the more experienced members until their clients discover their shortcomings. This is how networking organisations can, unwittingly, damage the profession and undermine the work of accrediting bodies.

W ell, from the records I found so far – birth certificates and that sort of thing – I think there's a very strong possibility that you are descended from royalty!

- 'Sir Francis Guesswork', 'leading family historian', speaking to King George IV in a take-off of Who Do You Think You Are? called 'George IV - Who on Earth Are You?', Horrible Histories (CBBC, Series 3, Episode 4, 2011)

On the other extreme there is the school of thought that equates education with academic qualifications. The last decades of the twentieth century did their best to eradicate the notion of 'learning on the job'. Either the job needed to be taught in a lecture theatre or it required no skills at all. That idea removed several professions from the workplace as a place of learning and brought extinction to several trades that were learnt entirely by apprenticeship.

Today, genealogy's long-felt inferiority complex (which will be touched on), coupled with heavily promoted academic courses, combine to create the perception that our field of study is in dire need of academic qualifications in order to be respected. Definitely there is a place for educational courses in genealogy, with or without certificates, diplomas or degrees. However, the idea that they are essential for all who seriously pursue ancestral research is blinkered, and it alienates whole sections of the worldwide family history community.

Between the disregard for accreditation on one side and the academic elitist movement on the other, professional credentials for genealogists are not being championed sufficiently. This book is an attempt in that direction.

The book is designed primarily for those working in, or entering, professional genealogy, but it should prove useful to clients in understanding the substance of claims made by any individuals they may think to engage. Clients may find SECTION 3 ('Developing a Career in Genealogical Research') informative. They might also refer to APPENDIX A ('Educational Opportunities for All') and APPENDIX C ('The Accrediting Bodies'). The Abbreviations section and the lists of general membership organisations in APPENDIX B also should prove useful.

All parts of the book are written with the professional genealogist in mind. Those in the early stages of their career may find particular interest in SECTION 3 ('Developing a Career in Genealogical Research'), APPENDIX A ('Educational Opportunities for All') and APPENDIX C ('The Accrediting Bodies'). Hopefully most practitioners will learn something of the background of their profession in SECTIONS 1 and 2, and find SECTIONS 4 and 5 thought-provoking at least.

In practice, our expertise is reflected in the quality of our output over time. Yet most potential clients lack adequate technical knowledge to distinguish us from those with fewer skills or a less developed sense of responsibility.

- *Donn Devine, 'Defining Professionalism', Professional Genealogy: a Manual for Researchers, Writers, Editors, Lecturers and Librarians, (Baltimore, Maryland 2001)*

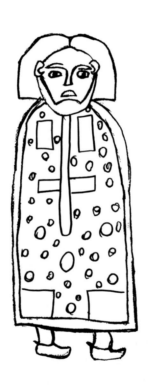

SECTION 1

The Development of Professional Genealogy and Credentials

THE DEVELOPMENT OF GENEALOGY AS A SERIOUS STUDY

Ancestral research as a serious pursuit has a long history. As early as 1834 a subscription periodical devoted in part to genealogy, *Collectanea Topographica et Genealogica*, was begun in England by John Gough Nichols (1806-1873). It ran into eight volumes, and was followed by other publications by Nichols, *The Topographer and Genealogist* and later *The Herald and Genealogist*. Anthony J. Camp, perhaps the most influential voice in British genealogy in the last quarter of the twentieth century, has stated that 'it is often said' that Nichols 'founded the modern critical and historical school of genealogy'. In 1853 the Genealogical and Historical Society of Great Britain was founded but it survived for little more than a decade. In the absence of a permanent ancestral research organisation, the subscription periodicals were the main focus for the serious genealogist.[1] In addition to periodicals devoted specifically to the subject, the learned journals of antiquarian and archaeological (otherwise historical) societies provided an outlet

---

[1] Anthony J. Camp, '150 Years of Genealogy', a talk given in 2013, http://anthonyjcamp.com/page18.htm, accessed 18 July 2018; Michael Sharpe, *Family Matters: A history of genealogy* (Barnsley, 2011), 73-74.

for scholarly articles on genealogical topics.

By the mid-nineteenth century genealogy also had started to develop in earnest in the USA. The New England Historic Genealogical Society, based in Boston, was founded in 1845 and it most likely was the first genealogical organisation in the world. Certainly it is now the oldest in the USA, followed by the New York Genealogical & Biographical Society, dating from 1869. From its inauguration the NYG&BS was open to female members, making it the first genealogical organisation in the USA to admit women. The quarterly periodicals, the *New England Historical & Genealogical Register* and the *New York Genealogical and Biographical Record*, have been published since 1847 and 1870, respectively.

In the United Kingdom, in 1869 Joseph Jackson Howard and George William Marshall were among the founders of the Harleian Society. It continues to this day, but as a publisher rather than a membership organisation. Its stated objectives are 'the transcribing, printing and publishing of the heraldic visitations of counties, parish registers or any manuscripts relating to genealogy, family history and heraldry'.

Howard began publication of the periodical *Miscellanea Genealogica et Heraldica* in 1866 and it lasted until 1938. Marshall began *The Genealogist* in 1877 and it survived until 1922. Anthony J. Camp commented that Marshall's *The Genealogist* 'received important critical contributions from ... the best genealogists of the time'.[2] In 1888 an early guide-book, *How to Write the History of a Family* by W.P.W. Phillimore, was published in London. Its second edition sold out within a few years and a *Supplement* appeared in 1896. Phillimore later founded his own genealogical publishing house.

An accurate proven pedigree which does not go beyond the last century is more creditable than a doubtful one three or four times as long ...

- *W.P.W. Phillimore, How to Write the History of a Family: A guide for the genealogist (London, 1888)*

---

[2] Camp, '150 Years'.

Anglophones are inclined to think of genealogy as originally a pursuit in English-speaking regions. In fact, the oldest existing genealogical organisation in Europe is Der Herold, founded in Berlin in 1869. It is a society for heraldry, genealogy and related sciences. Almost as old is *Heraldisch-Genealogischen Gesellschaft* «ADLER», which was founded in Vienna in 1870. The *Samfundet for Dansk-Norsk Genealogi og Personalhistorie* (Society for Danish-Norwegian Genealogy and Personal History) was founded in 1879. It began the biannual publication of its periodical, *Personalhistorisk Tidsskrift*, in 1880. In 1926 the society's name changed to *Samfundet for Dansk Genealogi og Personalhistorie*, when the separate *Norsk Slektshistorisk Forening* was established in Norway.

As well as organisations with primarily genealogical aims, there were historical societies that had a significant ancestral research element. These included the Huguenot societies founded in New York and London in the 1880s. Lineage societies were another type of organisation that developed in the late-nineteenth century. For instance, the Daughters of the American Revolution came into being in 1890, the Massachusetts Society of Mayflower Descendants in 1896, and the General Society of Mayflower Descendants in 1897.

Another early organisation specifically devoted to family history was the Genealogical Society of Pennsylvania, founded in 1892. It was followed two years later by the Genealogical Society of Utah (GSU), perhaps the most significant organisation in terms of its impact, but not a membership association as such. It was formed within the Church of Jesus Christ of Latter-day Saints (LDS Church). With the support of the church it developed the Family History Library in Salt Lake City, now the largest repository of genealogical material in the world. In the 1920s the GSU established a Research Bureau to assist church members tracing their ancestors.[3] The GSU should not be confused with the similarly named Utah Genealogical Association, a membership organisation founded in 1971. In the twenty-first century the public face of the GSU is FamilySearch International.

One of the last organisations to be established in the nineteenth century was the California Genealogical Society in 1898; one of the first in the twentieth century was the National Genealogical Society in Washington, DC, in 1903. The Society of Genealogists (SoG) was founded in London in 1911. It was followed by Finland's *Suomen Sukututkimusseura* in 1917, and the Genealogical Society of New Jersey in 1921.

---

[3] Jill N. Crandell, 'A Brief History of the Accreditation Program' in Kory L. Meyerink. Tristan L. Tolman and Linda K. Gulbrandsen, eds., *Becoming an Excellent Genealogist* [Kindle edn] (Salt Lake City, 2012).

One might wonder whether there were any professional genealogists involved in all this development, but they were present. Indeed, two of the main people involved in the founding of the SoG, George Sherwood and Charles Bernau, were professionals. In its first year the society numbered fourteen of its members who undertook professional research.[4]

It must be remembered that ancestral research was then the pursuit of those who were comfortably-off. Very many of the amateur genealogists who contributed to the administration of these societies, who conducted extensive research and who wrote scholarly articles, had private means and could afford to spend huge amounts of their time on family history. Those who conducted research for a fee often did so as a part-time occupation while pursuing a more lucrative career. In Ireland in the 1911 Census, Tenison Groves described himself as a 'Civil Engineer & Record Agent'; Gertrude Thrift described herself as a 'Genealogist and Drawing Teacher'; Mary Josephine O'Farrell was simply a 'Genealogist'.

Also in 1911, Sir Arthur Vicars, former Ulster King of Arms at Dublin's Office of Arms, then living in enforced retirement, described his occupation as 'Literary, Heraldic & Genealogical'. This is a reminder that those appointed as heralds in such institutions usually also practised as professional genealogists. The importance of the work of professional genealogical researchers in Ireland came to the fore following the destruction of the Public Record Office in 1922. Transcripts and abstracts made in the course of their work by professional researchers such as Tenison Groves and Gertrude Thrift and, to a lesser extent, Mary Josephine O'Farrell, helped to replace some of the lost material.

In 1922 a new privately produced periodical called the *New Haven Genealogical Magazine* was launched in the USA. The founder and editor was Donald Lines Jacobus (1887-1970), who stated his occupation as genealogist in the 1920, 1930 and 1940 US Federal Censuses. The magazine became very influential in ancestral research circles. It eventually became *The American Genealogist*, the name it continues under today. Through this periodical Jacobus strove to raise standards of scholarship within genealogy, and he had a major influence on how the serious study of genealogy evolved in the USA. In 1930 his book *Genealogy as Pastime and Profession* was published. Though written over 80 years ago, it contains some timeless truths about professional genealogy.

---

[4] I am indebted to Anthony J. Camp, former Director of the Society of Genealogists, for this information.

Conditions in the genealogical profession are unsatisfactory. They always have been unsatisfactory and will continue so unless some sort of association of genealogists shall one day be organized, limiting its membership to those whose competence has been proved.

- Donald Lines Jacobus, Genealogy as Pastime and Profession
(New Haven, Connecticut 1930)

Other genealogical societies were formed in various parts of the world in the first half of the twentieth century. The following is not an exhaustive list:

1932	Society of Australian Genealogists
1933	*Schweizerische Gesellschaft für Familienforschung* (Switzerland)
-	*Genealogiska Föreningen* (Sweden)
1936	Detroit Society for Genealogical Research (USA)
-	Irish Genealogical Research Society
1938	*Sällskapet Vallonättlingar* (Sweden)
1939	Wisconsin State Genealogical Society (USA)
1940	*Instituto Argentino de Ciencias Genealógicas* (Argentina)
1941	Genealogical Society of Victoria (Australia)
1943	*Société généalogique canadienne-française* (Canada)
1945	*Instituto Peruano de Investigaciones Genealógicas* (Peru)
1946	*Nederlandse Genealogische Vereniging* (Netherlands)
1948	*Instituto Chileno de Investigaciones Genealógicas* (Chile)
1950	*Colégio Brasileiro de Genealogia* (Brazil)

An organisation of a different kind was founded in 1940. This was the American Society of Genealogists (ASG). It differed in that it was an exclusive club for genealogists 'selected for the excellence and volume of their published works that would demonstrate ability to discover facts from original source material and to evaluate and present evidence'.[5] It was founded by Arthur Adams, Meredith Colket and John Insley Coddington, with membership confined to fifty life members, called Fellows. After the three founders, the fourth Fellow was Donald Lines Jacobus. The full complement of fifty Fellows was not achieved until 1944, after which election to fellowship was possible only as places arose due to death. Election was and is on the nomination of existing Fellows. As of May 2018 there have been a total of 167 individuals recognised as Fellows of the American Society of Genealogists. These have not been confined to Americans. For example, Sir Anthony Wagner from England was elected in 1944 and Sir Iain Moncreiffe of that Ilk from Scotland was elected in 1969.[6]

Though the ASG is not an organisation specifically for professional genealogists its stated aims include the advancing of standards in genealogical research and the gaining of recognition for genealogy 'as a serious subject of research in the historical and social fields of learning'.[7] Its biannual journal is *The Genealogist*. In addition it presents awards, scholarships and certificates of appreciation. In 1960 it published *Genealogical Research: Methods and Sources*, a handbook edited by Milton Rubincam with contributions from various Fellows.

Over half a century ago the ASG took two very significant steps towards raising standards. In 1950 it was instrumental in the establishment of the National Institute on Genealogical Research, an annual week-long intensive course on US federal records for experienced researchers, and the first of its kind. For professional genealogists the more significant step was in 1964, when the ASG created the Board for Certification of Genealogists (BCG).

THE HISTORY OF PROFESSIONAL CREDENTIALS IN GENEALOGY

1964 was indeed a very important year in the development of the profession. It saw the establishment of not just one but two processes for providing credentials for professional genealogists. At the same time as the Board for Certification of Genealogists was being formed by the American Society of Genealogists, the

---

[5] American Society of Genealogists, 'About the ASG > The First Fifty Years', http://fasg.org/about/first-fifty-years, accessed 18 July 2018.

[6] American Society of Genealogists, 'Fellows > All Fellows', http://fasg.org/fellows/all-fellows, accessed 18 July 2018.

[7] American Society of Genealogists, 'About the ASG', http://fasg.org/about, accessed 18 July 2018.

Genealogical Society of Utah was developing an alternative form of credential. These two processes introduced the terms Certified Genealogist and Accredited Genealogist into the vocabulary of family history in North America.

After almost four decades of serving LDS Church members, by the early 1960s the Genealogical Society of Utah's Research Bureau in Salt Lake City had become unable to cope with the increased demand for its services. The board of the GSU came to the decision that it would need to begin recommending professional researchers outside its bureau in order to relieve the pressure. To be in a position to recommend competent researchers the GSU needed to set some standards. In May 1963 it appointed Henry Christiansen and Frank Smith, two of its senior bureau staff, to draft testing guidelines for licensing external researchers in the Family History Library. The first person to receive the designation 'Accredited Genealogist' was Eric B. Christensen when he was accredited for Danish research in April 1964. By the end of the year 18 individuals had received accreditation. By the end of 1966 there were 88 Accredited Genealogists who collectively held 110 accreditations in 16 geographical testing areas.[8]

The evaluation process involved a four-generation research project, followed by an eight-hour written examination at the Family History Library in Salt Lake City, followed by an oral examination with a number of genealogists specialising in the geographical area for accreditation. The system of accreditation related, and still relates, to specific geographical areas. An individual may obtain accreditation for a number of regions, applying for each separately. Currently there are over 30 geographical areas available for testing worldwide. The vast majority of those seeking and obtaining the designation 'Accredited Genealogist' always have been resident in the USA, primarily accessing the records on microfilm through the Family History Library.

At about the same time as the Genealogical Society of Utah was developing its plans for credentials for professional researchers in Salt Lake City, the American Society of Genealogists was working along similar lines elsewhere in the USA. In October 1962 Jean Stephenson, the chairman of its Committee on Standards, reported that the Library of Congress and the National Archives in Washington, DC, suggested that some standard should be set by the ASG or the National Genealogical Society so that these institutions could be provided with a list of 'competent genealogists'. The ASG set up a Committee to Investigate Certification of Professional Genealogists. Its three members were Noel C.

[8] Crandell, 'A Brief History of the Accreditation Program'.

Stevenson, in the chair, Archibald F. Bennett and Jean Stephenson. The following year a board committee was appointed to carry out its recommendations. This Board of Genealogical Certification, which soon became the Board for Certification of Genealogists (BCG), held its first meeting in April 1964. Milton Rubincam was chairman of its Board of Trustees. In December 1964 he reported to the American Society of Genealogists that, while the ASG took the initiative in establishing BCG, it worked closely with officers of the National Genealogical Society, the New England Historic Genealogical Society and the Genealogical Society of Pennsylvania. He further stated that BCG was 'an independent body and not connected with any other organization'. Therefore, it had become an autonomous entity.[9]

BCG originally had two credential categories, those of Certified Genealogist (CG) and Certified Genealogical Record Searcher (CGRS). The first person to receive the designation 'Certified Genealogist' was Jean Stephenson herself, on 21 February 1965. Dr. Stephenson had been admitted a Fellow of the American Society of Genealogists in 1943 and had served as its Secretary. By the 1960s she had contributed to genealogy with distinction. She was central to the establishment of BCG and was on its Board of Trustees, but she still went through the assessment process to receive the designation 'Certified Genealogist' at the age of 72. She was one of a number of people who received certification on 21 February 1965. John Frederick Dorman, editor of *The Virginia Genealogist* from 1957, was the fourth person to obtain the designation that day. Like Jean Stephenson, he was a Fellow of the ASG and involved in establishing BCG, but he was a young man. He was still active as a CG at the start of the twenty-first century and in 2004 was awarded the status of BCG Emeritus Associate, which he still holds. The first person to receive the designation 'Certified Genealogical Record Searcher' (CGRS) was Sadye Giller on 6 August 1965.[10]

BCG's evaluation of applicants for its credential differed from that of the GSU, primarily in not having written and oral examinations for them to sit. BCG applicants were required to submit a range of material, including a report

---

[9] Crandell, 'A Brief History of the Accreditation Program'; Kay Haviland Freilich, 'BCG History', *OnBoard*, 7/1 (January 2001), www.bcgcertification.org/aboutbcg/bcghistory.html, accessed 28 February 2017 [no longer linked on page].

[10] Freilich, 'BCG History'; American Society of Genealogists, 'Fellows > All Fellows'; 'National Genealogy Hall of Fame Members' – Jean Stephenson, www.ngsgenealogy.org/cs/halloffame_winners, accessed 18 July 2018; Press Release, June 2012, re John Frederick Dorman, www.ngsgenealogy.org/galleries/press/FINAL__NGSJune_2012_Dorman_video_PR.pdf, accessed 18 July 2018.

prepared for a client, to demonstrate their all-round abilities.

Later new credential categories were introduced. These were Certified Genealogical Lecturer (CGL), Certified Genealogical Instructor (CGI), Certified American Lineage Specialist (CALS) and Certified American Indian Lineage Specialist (CAILS). By the end of the twentieth century the CALS and CAILS categories had been merged as Certified Lineage Specialist (CLS). In 2005 the three research credentials, CG, CGRS and CLS, were merged. Those holding them thereafter became Certified Genealogists, and BCG established new requirements for the single designation. While the various categories had their different roles, it was felt that the distinctions were not well understood, both within genealogy and with the general public. More recently one of the teaching categories, CGI, was discontinued, so that now there are only two credentials, Certified Genealogist and Certified Genealogical Lecturer.[11]

The first trustees of BCG were to serve one to three years, with five new people appointed each year, elected by the current trustees, keeping the number at fifteen. At the end of the twentieth century a change was made, allowing those currently certified by BCG to vote for trustees. By then 425 researchers had received the designation CG and 805 had been designated CGRS.[12]

Two significant publications have been produced by BCG. In 2000 *The BCG Genealogical Standards Manual* appeared, 'designed to clarify, codify, and organize standards generally accepted in the field'. BCG's more recent book, *Genealogy Standards*, published in 2014, is a revised edition of the *Manual*, updating, expanding and clarifying its approach to research standards. In addition, *The BCG Application Guide* may be downloaded for free from its website. BCG now recognises former CGs who have retired from professional research. Emeritus Associate status may be offered at the discretion of the trustees to those with a long and distinguished career with BCG who are retired or semi-retired. Retired Associate status is offered to those who have retired having been certified for more than twenty years.

In 1999 the Genealogical Society of Utah considered ending its involvement with providing the credential 'Accredited Genealogist'. It arranged with BCG to allow Accredited Genealogists the option of transferring to become Certified Genealogists instead. The GSU also asked the Utah Genealogical Association (UGA) to consider the creation of an organisation to continue the work of

---

[11] Freilich, 'BCG History'.
[12] Freilich, 'BCG History'.

accreditation. In February 2000 the UGA appointed an Accreditation Committee which developed into the International Commission for the Accreditation of Professional Genealogists (ICAPGen). The three members of this committee and first Commission were Jimmy B. Parker, in the chair, Ray T. Clifford and Jill N. Crandell. The Commission was supported by an advisory committee with four members, Karen A. Clifford, Louise LaCount, Kory L. Meyerink and George R. Ryskamp. In August 2000 the Genealogical Society of Utah officially transferred responsibility for accreditation to ICAPGen. In the 36 years during which the GSU ran the accreditation programme it approved 477 individuals as Accredited Genealogists. Testing under ICAPGen began in October 2000.[13]

In 2002 ICAPGen introduced Emeritus status for retiring AGs 'in good standing'. To facilitate applicants for accreditation based outside Utah, ICAPGen initially added two alternative examination locations, the Genealogy Department of the Allen County Public Library at Fort Wayne, Indiana, and the Daughters of the American Revolution Library in Washington, DC. Now arrangements can be made to sit the examination in locations near the applicant's residence. In 2012 ICAPGen published *Becoming an Excellent Genealogist: Essays on Professional Research Skills*, edited by three AGs, Kory L. Meyerink, Tristan L. Tolman and Linda K. Gulbrandsen. ICAPGen's *Guide to Applying for an Accredited Genealogist® Credential* may be downloaded for free from its website.

Both the Accredited Genealogist and Certified Genealogist / Certified Genealogical Lecturer credentials last only five years and must be renewed continually throughout a researcher's career. The accrediting processes which came into existence since 1964 in other parts of the world do not impose such restrictions on credentials. However, as with most professions, they now generally expect those accredited to partake in continuing professional development (CPD).

British Isles

Back in the 1960s, on the other side of the Atlantic, professional credentials also were being considered. The idea of forming an association for professional genealogists and record agents in England was conceived by Philip Haslewood Blake in 1962, during his short tenure as Director of Research at the Society of Genealogists. The SoG had an established research department that conducted searches in London record repositories, with only occasional visits to county record offices, while very little work was sub-contracted out. As Secretary of the

---

[13] Crandell, 'A Brief History of the Accreditation Program'.

SoG the previous year, Blake had initiated the engagement of researchers outside London to conduct parish register searches. This new departure was continued and developed by his successor as Director of Research, Anthony J. Camp, who drew up lists of researchers arranged by area and expertise. Gaining first-hand knowledge of the work of various researchers throughout England, Camp became aware of a significant disparity in ability between individual practitioners. He felt there was a need for an organisation to provide a list of recommended researchers.[14]

Very few professional genealogists are deliberately fraudulent, but many are so naive or careless or haphazard in their work that the results are fully as bad.

- Donald Lines Jacobus, Genealogy as Pastime and Profession
(New Haven, Connecticut 1930)

Having left the SoG in 1963, Blake pursued his idea of an association. According to Anthony J. Camp, Blake's 'continual interest, pressure and critical input' made it succeed. He initiated a series of meetings with other interested parties. The first took place on 6 July 1967 at the office of the genealogical firm of Brooks, Davies & Foster Ltd., 5 Fenchurch Street, London. It was attended by Blake, Camp, Brian G.C. Brooks (managing director of the host company), A. Noel Currer-Briggs (known for his books on settlers in Virginia), Terrick V.H. Fitzhugh (founding editor of *The Amateur Historian*, the forerunner of *The Local Historian*) and Malcolm Pinhorn (former director of Phillimore & Co. Ltd.).[15]

A year later, on 24 June 1968, the inaugural meeting of the Association of Genealogists and Record Agents (AGRA) was held at the Stationers' Hall in London, with 21 people in attendance. Articles of association were agreed and officers elected. Sir Gyles Isham was appointed President, and the other officers

---

[14] Information supplied by Anthony J. Camp.
[15] Information supplied by Anthony J. Camp; 'Terrick Fitzhugh: an appreciation', *The Local Historian*, 22/1 (February 1992), 6-7.

were Brooks (Chairman), Currer-Briggs (Secretary) and Pinhorn (Treasurer), while Camp, Fitzhugh and Patrick Smythe-Wood formed the council.[16] AGRA took a very different approach to those of the two American organisations. Firstly, those admitted became members of the association, rather than being accredited or certified by a board. Secondly, membership was initially by invitation, based on reputation, rather like the approach of the American Society of Genealogists.

The invitations were based largely on the lists developed at the Society of Genealogists and the first people approached to join were personally known to Council members. In most cases they could be recommended as having been engaged by at least one of them for research over a number of years. From its early days AGRA published a List of Members. The 1973 edition stated that membership was 'open only to well qualified persons of considerable practical experience and members have for the most part been actively engaged as genealogists or record agents for a number of years'. While the first Members were admitted on reputation, not all genealogical researchers were known to the founding Council. The application form for genealogists used before 1977 requested the applicant's qualifications and years of practice, and details of extensive experience had to be provided, along with samples of their work. In addition, the names and addresses of three referees were required. The referees had to be people who knew the applicant's professional work and who could vouch for their ability and integrity.[17]

Contrary to one assessment of AGRA as being 'little more than another club – a closed shop even – for those at the top of the profession',[18] it was by no means elitist or exclusive: by 1974 there were 63 members. It was, and is, open to professional genealogists throughout the British Isles but now applications are confined to those conducting research in English or Welsh records. AGRA has had members from all countries of the United Kingdom, as well as the Republic of Ireland. In the 1980s it even had one Member in France. This was Margaret Audin, an Englishwoman who lived permanently in Paris.

A formal complaints procedure was approved in 1971. A sub-committee was appointed to oversee it. A code of practice was first formally adopted in 1972 and it was revised several times thereafter. From 1977, for the first time, record agents had to provide at least one sample of work, which had to be in the form of a report commissioned by a client. By 1985 the AGRA List of Members stated that

---

[16] Information from Anthony J. Camp; *AGRA Newsletter,* 84 (2008), 9.
[17] Information from Anthony J. Camp; *AGRA Newsletter,* 84 (2008), 9.
[18] Sharpe, *Family Matters,* 156.

Members had 'proved their professional competence upon application' and this statement continued in use until 2001.[19]

In 1991 AGRA introduced the new category of Affiliate Member for those working towards gaining full membership, but Affiliates were not allowed to advertise this status. In 2007 the rules were changed and they were permitted to use the term 'AGRA Affiliate'. A further change took place in 2011, when Affiliate status was changed to that of Associate membership. Since 2015 Associates have been allowed a profile page on the AGRA website, whereas previously only their contact details were given.

The association announced in 1995 that awards from the Institute of Heraldic and Genealogical Studies in Canterbury would be 'accepted for entry into AGRA when adequate evidence of experience and professional acumen is demonstrated'.[20] The Institute's courses in genealogy and heraldry came with a certificate or qualification.

About the same time there was an extraordinary attack on both the profession and AGRA by one of its own members who, in fact, was the founder of the Institute. In May 1995 an article appeared in *The Times* quoting Cecil Humphery-Smith as claiming that clients were 'being taken for a ride', with dishonest practitioners charging exorbitant rates, selling the same research twice and exaggerating the amount of research needed to obtain information. He was quoted as saying that it was important that genealogists be governed by a proper professional body. Quite understandably AGRA's then chairman, Beryl Crawley, was reported as taking exception to this. The article also stated that most genealogists had 'no formal qualifications'. This was inaccurate, of course, as membership of AGRA was a qualification in the form of accreditation. But, as the courses run by Humphery-Smith's Institute were the only other source of 'qualifications' at the time, it is possible to speculate about the cause of the outburst.[21]

In 2001 the association changed its name to the Association of Genealogists and Researchers in Archives, but retained the acronym AGRA. The change was an attempt to encourage those researchers from a wider range of disciplines to join. While the membership list on AGRA's website once differentiated between genealogists, record agents and those from specialist categories, this was changed in order to offer lists of members categorised by expertise. From

---

[19] Information from Anthony J. Camp.
[20] *AGRA Newsletter*, 54 (1995), 4-5.
[21] Edward Gorman, 'Genealogists are told to put their house in order', *The Times*, 22 May 1995, 5.

2001 until September 2014, membership applications could be made as either a Genealogist or a Research Specialist. The latter category allowed for researchers specialising in such areas as tracing living relatives, military or railway records, or chancery proceedings, while applications were welcomed from researchers with considerable experience as translators, historians or librarians.

AGRA entered a formal partnership with the Association of Scottish Genealogists and Researchers in Archives (ASGRA) in 2010. The following year AGRA established its Fellowship to recognise outstanding contribution by members. In September 2014 the application criteria for Members and Associates were altered in favour of those having attended courses run by the Institute of Heraldic and Genealogical Studies and the University of Strathclyde, and to encourage continuing professional development (CPD), while references as to the applicant's personal integrity were replaced by an interview. The category of Research Specialist was discontinued from that time. AGRA now has only Members and Associates. In June 2018 the advanced certificate course run jointly by Pharos and the Society of Genealogists was added to the educational options considered in AGRA's application criteria.

Australasia

Credentials for professional genealogists were first introduced in the southern hemisphere in the 1970s. Before there was any move to establish an accrediting body, the Society of Australian Genealogists (SAG) in Sydney began a Diploma in Family Historical Studies (DipFHS). This was restricted to its members but it became an accepted path for professional genealogists.

The 1st Australasian Congress on Genealogy and Heraldry was held in Melbourne in April 1977 and was attended by enthusiasts from throughout Australia and New Zealand. One of the outcomes of it was the formation of the Australasian Federation of Family History Organisations, which was launched the following year in Canberra. Another was the establishment of the Australasian Association of Genealogists and Record Agents (AAGRA). It was launched in Melbourne at a meeting on 12 April 1977, during the Congress.

AAGRA's first Chairman was Lorne Henry Greville, the Honorary Secretary was Evelyn Brown and the other Council members were Kingsley Ireland, Brian Croker and Donald Grant.[22] It would appear that AAGRA styled itself on the British AGRA, having asked for and received copies of its application form,

---

[22] I am grateful to Faye M. Young, MAAGRA, for this information.

code of practice and constitution. In 1978 AAGRA communicated with AGRA, requesting some type of affiliation. AGRA suggested an exchange of newsletters and requested a membership list but no actual link was established between the two organisations.[23] AAGRA's first newsletter appeared in May 1979.

AAGRA's Council approached twenty likely candidates for membership and by the end of March 1980 there were eleven members. Whatever the initial criteria were for application, by 1981 candidates had to provide supporting information, such as evidence of dealings with clients and the authorship of publications.[24]

As of 1986 there were 29 Members of AAGRA, spread through New South Wales, Queensland, South Australia, Tasmania, Victoria, Western Australia and New Zealand. Membership applications had to be written in a prescribed form for the consideration of AAGRA's council. Record agents had to submit evidence that they knew the available records and their location, that they were capable of searching them, making a coherent report to a client and quoting references. Genealogists had to submit evidence, preferably in published form, that they were capable of conducting full research, with charts and complete references, that they had the ability to relate the subject matter to its historical context, and that they could write a coherent report. If applicants had any formal qualification, such as the SAG Diploma in Family Historical Studies, they were to present details. Applications could be made for either record agent or genealogist category, or both. If admitted, they had to subscribe to AAGRA's Code of Ethics.[25]

An advertisement for AAGRA, including its membership list, was published in the 1989 edition of the *Genealogical Research Directory*.[26] It stated that membership was 'open only to well qualified persons of considerable practical experience in the fields of genealogy & record searching'. It indicated that a genealogist 'compiles family histories & genealogies for clients & often is also responsible for effecting the publication of the finished project'. On the other hand, a record agent 'specialises in the knowledge of records & sources, & the researching of these'. At that point AAGRA had 32 members: three of them were classed as genealogists only; ten were both genealogists and record agents; while 19 were record agents

---

[23] I am grateful to Ian Marson, FGRA, past Chairman of AGRA, for this information.

[24] Information from Faye M. Young, MAAGRA.

[25] Faye M. Young, 'The Role of the Professional Genealogist in Australia', in Geoffrey Burkhardt and Peter Procter, eds., *Bridging the Generations: Fourth Australasian Congress on Genealogy and Heraldry*, Canberra 1986 (Canberra, 1986), 441-2.

[26] Keith A. Johnson and Malcolm R. Sainty (eds.): *Genealogical Research Directory National & International*, 1989, 823.

only. Ten of the members held the SAG Diploma in Family Historical Studies.

Unlike AGRA and the Scottish organisation, ASGRA, AAGRA has retained its original name and its two categories of membership, those of genealogist and record agent. The abbreviated definition of these currently on its website has a slightly different wording. It states that a genealogist 'manages research projects and compiles family histories and genealogies for clients', while a record agent 'specialises in the research of specific records and/or the holdings of specific archives'. Its information on membership application gives a definition similar to the earlier wording.

Because of the vast geographical area it covers its Members rarely have the opportunity to meet face-to-face. The only event guaranteed to gather most serious genealogists together in that region is the Australasian Congress on Genealogy and Heraldry, which is held every three years. Because of these difficulties, AAGRA's annual general meeting now is held by teleconference.

AAGRA has made some significant changes in recent years. In November 2015 its constitution was altered, its new format being based loosely on the model rules for an association promoted by Consumer Affairs Victoria. One of the changes allowed for Members to use the post-nominal initials MAAGRA. At the same time the association's senior officer was changed from Chairman to President, while two additional membership categories were introduced; Associate Member for those working towards gaining full membership, and Fellow, recognising outstanding contribution by Members.

Scotland

The Association of Scottish Genealogists and Record Agents (ASGRA) came into existence in 1981, again providing credentials similar to AGRA's for professional researchers in Scotland. In January 1981 it was reported at an AGRA Council meeting that Sheila Pitcairn, AGRA's only Member in Scotland, had informed the association about a proposed body for Scottish professional genealogists. The Council understood the reason for the new organisation and agreed that AGRA was not then equipped to represent Scottish genealogists. It was further agreed that goodwill and assistance would be offered, with the hope that if the new body was formed there would be close links and co-operation between the two.[27]

The initial meeting of the new Scottish organisation was held on 22 January 1981. It was agreed that membership would be open to well-qualified researchers

[27] Information from Ian Marson, FGRA.

with considerable practical experience. The first officers were elected on 19 May 1981. They were Donald Whyte (President), Rosemary Bigwood (Chairman), Sheila Pitcairn (Secretary) and David Burns (Treasurer).[28]

In January 1982 AGRA's Council again discussed ASGRA. It was open to the possibility of the new organisation dealing with most matters relating to Scottish researchers, while AGRA would not entirely relinquish responsibility for Scotland. The following month ASGRA more precisely defined that membership would be open to 'experienced and well-qualified professional researchers working personally in Scotland'. Later that year AGRA became aware that the Scottish body did not intend to make a distinction between genealogists and record agents, assuming that all its Members practised in both capacities. This was because Scottish records were generally centralised. For that reason ASGRA was limiting its membership to those researching within Scotland and not entertaining applications from genealogists directing research from elsewhere. Up to that point AGRA apparently considered the possibility of a form of reciprocal membership, with ASGRA Members also listed by AGRA. This was no longer considered.[29]

It appears that for the first year ASGRA may not have required submission of sample reports for evaluation, but from January 1982 samples were submitted. The association's first newsletter, published the following month, reported that there were fourteen Members. By May there were twenty. Membership applications have always been assessed by a panel of Members. At the annual general meeting in 1988 it was agreed that a new Code of Practice, a new constitution and new requirements for applicants would be drafted. From about that time an Associate Member category was available for Members who chose not to be available for commission or those in employment outside the terms defined for a genealogist or record agent. To re-activate full membership the Associate was obliged to submit research reports for evaluation.[30]

ASGRA's rules have evolved over the years. In 1985 membership applicants were required to have practised for two years and to have attended classes in genealogy as well as the handwriting course then run by the Scottish Record Office. In 1993 applicants were required to have practised for two years full-time or four years part-time in genealogy. Membership requirements were

---

[28] I am grateful to Janet Bishop, FSGRA, Chairman of ASGRA, for this information.
[29] Information from AGRA and ASGRA Council minutes, per Ian Marson, FGRA, and Janet Bishop, FSGRA.
[30] Information from ASGRA Council minutes, per Janet Bishop, FSGRA.

considered again in 1997 and at an extraordinary general meeting some proposals were discussed. One was to introduce a category for those working towards membership. This resulted in the first two Probationers being admitted in 2000. A Specialist Member category was also in operation about that time but it fell into disuse over a decade ago.

In 1988 Malcolm Innes of Edingight, Lord Lyon King of Arms, consented to be Patron of ASGRA. His successors have continued in that role, with the present Lord Lyon, Joseph Morrow being ASGRA's current Patron. Donald Whyte remained President until his death in 2010. The position remained vacant until the appointment of Alan MacLeod in 2015.

ASGRA joined the Scottish Association of Family History Societies in December 1993. It changed its name to the Association of Scottish Genealogists and Researchers in Archives in 2004, but retained the acronym ASGRA. After having contact at the time of its foundation with AGRA, it was not until 2010 that the two organisations entered into a formal partnership. In April 2016 ASGRA also entered an alliance with Accredited Genealogists Ireland.

A new departure came in 2013, when ASGRA agreed to guarantee acceptance at Probationer level of those awarded the post-graduate diploma from the University of Strathclyde from July 2013 forward. In order to ensure that Strathclyde's certificate and diploma courses continued to meet ASGRA's requirements, an ASGRA appointee was to serve on the University's Genealogical Studies board. The acceptance facility has been since extended to holders of Strathclyde's certificate (backdated to 2012), while other arrangements were made for those holding older diplomas. Diplomas from Strathclyde are now accepted as partially fulfilling the requirements for ASGRA membership. From April 2015 ASGRA has had a somewhat similar arrangement for those holding certificates or diplomas from the University of Dundee.

In July 2015 a new category of Affiliate was introduced to allow for mutually relevant and beneficial association with individuals not practising as genealogists. In December 2015 ASGRA appointed an external assessment moderator and a systems and procedures advisor. The most recent development was in February 2017, when ASGRA established its Fellowship to recognise outstanding contribution by members.

Atlantic Canada

The 1980s saw the formation of two more regional accrediting bodies, one in Canada and the other in Ireland. The Genealogical Institute of the Maritimes (GIM) was established in 1983. GIM is a federally-incorporated body. It was founded under the auspices of the Council of Maritime Premiers, an agency formed in the early 1970s for co-operation between the three Maritime provinces of Canada – New Brunswick, Nova Scotia and Prince Edward Island. These three, along with the adjacent mainland province of Newfoundland, form Atlantic Canada.

According to its website, GIM came about in response to the need, as perceived by leading genealogists, genealogical societies and archivists, for credentials for genealogical researchers serving the public. The initiative was taken by the Provincial Archivists of the three Maritime provinces, who wished to have a list of reliable genealogical researchers to recommend to the general public. The six founding Members were Ann Coles and Allan MacRae of Prince Edward Island, Robert Fellows and Stephen White of New Brunswick, and Terrence Punch and Allan Marble of Nova Scotia. Though interest was expressed from Newfoundland to form a fourth region under the coverage of GIM, this was not accepted due to conditions at that time. It was felt that transportation difficulties would prevent provincial representatives from Newfoundland from attending the organisation's six-monthly executive meetings. However, in 1986 Newfoundland was added to GIM's area.[31]

GIM has always had two categories: Genealogical Record Searcher and Certified Genealogist. The latter is referred to as Certified Genealogist [Canada] to distinguish it from the similarly named American credential, issued by the Board for Certification of Genealogists. Those admitted to accreditation become Members of GIM. The application and assessment processes have remained unchanged since the organisation's foundation. GIM has examined individuals from other provinces of Canada in cases where the application is in relation to the genealogical sources of Atlantic Canada.

Quebec

Another Canadian accrediting body was started in 1991 by the *Fédération québécoise des sociétés de généalogie* (FQSG). In 1965 the *Fédération des sociétés d'histoire du Québec* was

---

[31] I am grateful to Allan Marble, CG(C), for this information.

founded. It had a genealogical council, and in March 1984 this was incorporated as a separate entity as FQSG. Then on 20 April 1991 FQSG established the *Bureau québécois d'attestation de compétence en généalogie* (BQACG). While any changes to accreditation rules go before a general meeting of the FQSG, the bureau exercises full autonomy in evaluation of applications for certification.

There are three levels of credentials under the BQACG. These are, in ascending order, *Généalogiste de filiation agréé* (GFA – Certified Lineage Genealogist), *Généalogiste recherchiste agréé* (GRA – Certified Genealogical Researcher) and *Maître généalogiste agréé* (MGA – Certified Master Genealogist). Between spring 2011 and spring 2016 the Bureau accredited 33 GFAs, four GRAs and two MGAs.[32] During 2016 it accredited one GFA.[33]

Ireland

Up to the early 1980s the majority of Irish genealogical records were accessible only in repositories in Dublin and Belfast. For that reason professional genealogists were based around these cities. In the early 1980s there were no more than about twenty professional researchers between both locations. A number of those in Belfast were attached to the Ulster Historical Foundation, then the research wing of the Public Record Office of Northern Ireland. In Dublin, most, like myself, were members of the panel of freelance researchers engaged by the Genealogical Office. The Genealogical Office, otherwise known as the Office of the Chief Herald, in Dublin Castle, was the state agency with responsibility for genealogy and heraldry. It has been reduced since to a section of the National Library of Ireland.

About that time the idea of providing some form of credential for professional genealogists was mooted by the then Chief Herald, Donal Begley, but this was superseded by developments in Northern Ireland. It was at the instigation of the Belfast-based researchers that an accrediting organisation was formed in 1986. An initial meeting of local researchers was held in Belfast on 11 March 1986 and a steering committee was appointed. On 13 May 1986 the steering committee's proposals were adopted at a general meeting at 121 Saintfield Road, Belfast, then the home of David McElroy, who was a Member of AGRA. Thus the Association of Professional Genealogists *of* Ireland (APGI) was born.

---

[32] 'Rapport annuel de la présidente 2015-2016', http://federationgenealogie.qc.ca/federation/rapport-annuel, accessed 10 March 2017 [no longer linked on page].

[33] 'Rapport annuel de la présidente 2016-2017', http://federationgenealogie.qc.ca/federation/rapport-annuel, accessed 6 June 2017 [no longer linked on page].

Little thought was given to the mode of accreditation and initially it was decided that anyone already accredited by AGRA would be admitted automatically, and that they would assess other applicants. At this early stage some researchers refused to submit material for assessment and they set up a separate non-accrediting representative organisation which apparently still operates as the Association of Ulster Genealogists and Record Agents. The new APGI continued its work and altered its name slightly to Association of Professional Genealogists *in* Ireland. I first heard of this grouping on a visit to Belfast sometime in the summer of 1986. The organisers were anxious for the Dublin-based researchers to form a parallel body in Dublin so that APGI would cover all of Ireland.

A general meeting of Dublin-area professional researchers was held at Adelaide Road, Dublin, then a temporary base for the Genealogical Office. Anyone known to be involved in professional research was invited to attend. John McCabe of APGI came along to explain the progress made in Belfast. The feeling of this meeting was that membership of AGRA could not be a criterion for membership of any new organisation and that applications would have to be vetted by an independent panel of assessors. A steering committee was appointed. It approached a number of people knowledgeable on genealogical research and sources who were not practising professional researchers, asking them to act as assessors. The first four members of what became the Board of Assessors were Gerard Slevin, former Chief Herald (Chairman), Donal Begley, the then Chief Herald, Aideen Ireland, archivist at the then Public Record Office of Ireland, and Beryl Phair (née Eustace), who had been a professional genealogists from the late 1920s.

An initial meeting took place in Dublin in November 1986 between the assessors, the steering committee and a representative of the Belfast group. Further meetings took place in early 1987. The Dublin steering committee visited Belfast in February 1987 to meet what was then called the Ulster Section of APGI. It was agreed then that the members of the Ulster Section would submit reports to be vetted by the independent assessors.

During 1987 the independent assessors began examining applications from Dublin-based applicants. The first seven applicants approved for membership of what was called the Dublin Section held their first general meeting on 16 October 1987. I was privileged to be one of them. The Ulster and Dublin Sections operated as separate branches of APGI, with their own committees, until the organisation's first annual general meeting in December 1988. At the proposal of the Ulster Section it was agreed that from that time forward APGI would function as a united organisation under a single council. The first President was Eilish Ellis. The joint Patrons were Donal Begley, Chief Herald of Ireland, and John Brooke-Little, Norroy and Ulster King of Arms, who held heraldic jurisdiction over Northern Ireland. Both retired from office in 1995 and the role of Patron was left in abeyance from that point.

APGI obtained permission from AGRA to style its constitution on AGRA's, with amendments. From its inception APGI has had only one category of membership, regarding that of 'record agent' as not likely to be attractive to applicants. Over the years APGI modified its application process, particularly since having contact in the 2010s with AGRA and ASGRA. Fellowship was introduced in 2004, while Affiliate status was sanctioned in December 2012 and an Emeritus Member category was established in December 2015.

In May 2015, at an extraordinary general meeting APGI changed its name. This mainly was due to its identity being confused with that of the non-accrediting American networking group called the Association of Professional Genealogists (APG). In recent years APG had begun in earnest to recruit members from outside North America and as a result the name APGI was progressively losing its significance. APGI became Accredited Genealogists Ireland (AGI), a name that reflects its primary function of providing accreditation. In April 2016 AGI entered an alliance with ASGRA.

France

Outside the English-speaking world and Quebec it appears that only France has a system of credentials for professional genealogists. This is dissimilar to the systems operating elsewhere. In France a differentiation is made between the *généalogiste familial* (who conducts traditional genealogical research) and the *généalogiste successoral* (who conducts genealogical research related to probate or inheritance and who works closely with a notary). There are far more *généalogistes successoraux* than *généalogistes familiaux*, and the former are obliged by law to hold a licence in order to gain access to certain records. They are required to be part of a professional chamber or association (*syndicat*), which in turn is part of a national union of associations formed in 2004.

The *Union des Syndicats de Généalogistes Professionnels* (USGP) was formed in 2004 by three professional chambers: the *Syndicat National des Généalogistes* (SNG), the *Chambre Syndicale des Généalogistes et Héraldistes de France* (CSGHF) and the *Chambre des Généalogistes Professionnels* (CGP). To complicate matters, two of these three changed their names in more recent times. In December 2011 SNG became the *Chambre Nationale des Généalogistes* (CNG). In January 2015 CSGHF became SYGENE, *l'Alliance des généalogistes professionnels*.

In 2008 USGP signed a partnership with the *Conseil Supérieur du Notariat*, a body established in 1945, representing notaries throughout France. The partnership was renewed in May 2015. By 2014 the USGP had two additional professional chambers: the *Chambre des Généalogistes Successoraux de France* (CGSF) and the *Compagnie Européenne des Généalogistes Successoraux* (CEGS). To confuse matters further, in April 2015 USGP, the national union of associations, became simply *Généalogistes de France*. This umbrella body now has six member chambers or associations:

> *Chambre des Généalogistes Professionnels* (CGP)
> *Chambre des Généalogistes Successoraux de France* (CGSF)
> *Chambre Internationale des Généalogistes Professionnels* (CIGP)
> *Chambre Syndicale des Généalogistes de France* (CSGF)
> *Compagnie Européenne des Généalogistes Successoraux* (CEGS)
> SYGENE

According to its website, *Généalogistes de France* represents 95% of those working in France as either *généalogistes familiaux* or *généalogistes successoraux*.[34] An individual cannot apply directly to *Généalogistes de France* to become a member: they must join one of its six associations. The associations appear mainly to list companies rather than individuals as members, but *Généalogistes de France* issues professional cards to individuals belonging to the associations and maintains an online list of the cards-holders, indicating their company and their association.[35] The six chambers or associations apparently have similar application criteria in terms of eligibility and similar vetting processes. The individual genealogist must decide which to apply to, though only SYGENE and CGP represent *généalogistes familiaux*.

Both *Généalogistes de France* and its six member associations seem to fulfil a role somewhere between the accrediting bodies in other jurisdictions and the

---

[34] Généalogistes de France, 'Présentation de l'Union', http://genealogistes-france.org/qui-sommes-nous/presentation-de-lunion, accessed 18 July 2018.

[35] Généalogistes de France, 'Liste des titulaires de la carte professionnelle', http://genealogistes-france.org/qui-sommes-nous/liste-des-titulaires-de-la-carte-professionnelle, accessed 18 July 2018.

non-accrediting support / networking groups (see below). In common with the accrediting and non-accrediting organisations, the French bodies expect their adherents to respect *Généalogistes de France*'s code of practice, the *Charte déontologique des généalogistes professionnels*. While they do not appear to have any formal accreditation processes, they provide an assurance of the competence of their adherents. In December 2016, at the suggestion of *Généalogistes de France*, the national commission for consumer mediation appointed Gérard Gaucher as ombudsman for the professional genealogy sector.

TOWARDS ACCREDITATION FOR GERMAN SPEAKERS

Verband deutschsprachiger Berufsgenealogen (the Association of German-Speaking Professional Genealogists) does not claim to be an accrediting organisation, but its practices are quite close to those of most organisations providing credentials. It was founded in September 1992 in Berlin. It is committed to mandatory standards, diligent processing of requests and production of verifiable reports with comprehensive referencing. *Verband deutschsprachiger Berufsgenealogen* serves professional genealogists working in areas in which German is, or has been, spoken. To be eligible for membership the applicant must be earning at least part of their income from genealogical research.[36]

Becoming a member is not just a matter of payment of a fee. The organisation is currently working on an accreditation system. As matters stand, an applicant must submit a sample research report. If this is considered to be of a sufficient standard the applicant is asked to attend an interview at which they are questioned on relevant topics, such as the ability to read old German script and knowledge of sources and archives in their specified region. Usually two of those conducting the interview specialise in that region.[37]

ACCREDITATION FOR LEGAL MATTERS

Legal or probate genealogists, also sometimes called heir searchers or heir locators, have been part of professional genealogy for over a century. Their work very often goes way beyond the area of wills or the identification of heirs. Perhaps the term 'legal genealogist' is the most accurate for the specialty, as it

---

[36] Verband deutschsprachiger Berufsgenealogen, 'Articles of Association', www.berufsgenealogie.net/english/files/Articles-of-Association.pdf, accessed 18 July 2018.
[37] I am grateful to Andrea Bentschneider, Chairwoman of Verband deutschsprachiger Berufsgenealogen, for this information.

encompasses work in all areas in which genealogy comes in contact with the law. There is a need for genealogical research for legal matters in all jurisdictions. A practitioner's competence for producing evidence, perhaps, is determined differently in different countries. In regions where accreditation is available from a relevant body (i.e. Australasia, France, Ireland, North America and the United Kingdom) such accreditation, indicating experience and competence, has long been be a sufficient credential for the legal system. Indeed, for those without professional credentials, experience and a reputation built up over many years may suffice in many cases.

As mentioned above, in France *généalogistes successoraux* are obliged by law to hold a licence in order to gain access to certain records, and they must be part of a professional chamber or association, which in turn is part of *Généalogistes de France*. There is no such regulation in most countries. In the United Kingdom there are many probate researchers and firms and there are competing support organisations, such as the Federation of Probate and Asset Researchers (FPAR), representing sections of the business. However, many researchers are not members of any of them. To a great extent FPAR's membership is made up of smaller probate firms and sole traders. Recently two of the larger companies of probate researchers formed rival organisations purporting to represent the interests of probate researchers in the UK.

In the past decade a new expression has entered the genealogical arena in the USA, causing some confusion and controversy. According to Barbara Jean Mathews in a 2012 post to her blog *The Demanding Genealogist*, the term 'forensic genealogy' was coined by Colleen Fitzpatrick. Fitzpatrick, a genealogist and former nuclear physicist, published her book *Forensic Genealogy* in 2005. On her website Fitzpatrick states:

In explaining how to analyze photographs, to mine databases, and to use DNA analysis to reveal family history, Forensic Genealogy emphasizes the creative parts of an investigation over the mechanics.

In an interview with *The Demanding Genealogist* in 2012 she stated:

Forensic Genealogy has been called "CSI meets Roots". It is the application of forensic investigative techniques to solving genealogical mysteries.[38]

More recently, in an interview published in October 2016 in the Polish

---

[38] Forensic Genealogy, 'What is Forensic Genealogy?', www.forensicgenealogy.info/index.html, accessed 18 July 2018; Barbara Jean Mathews, "A Response to 'What Is Forensic Genealogy?'", *The Demanding Genealogist*, posted 23 May 2012, http://demandinggenealogist.blogspot.com/2012/05/response-to-what-is-forensic-genealogy.html, accessed 18 July 2018.

online genealogical magazine *More Maiorum*, Fitzpatrick stated:

Genealogists have assisted attorneys with probate matters and searching for missing heirs for a long time. It was only in 2005 when I published Forensic Genealogy *that the term was first used to describe the application of scientific techniques to solving genealogical mysteries. Since then, the term "forensic genealogy" has taken on a more formal legal context.*

In the interview, she went on to define her coined phrase more succinctly:

Forensic genealogy is the application of genealogical research to support the legal identification process.

Asked about what conventional genealogy and 'forensic genealogy' have in common, she stated:

Forensic genealogy and traditional genealogy both use the same resources and techniques for researching kinship. These include photo analysis, database mining and DNA analysis. The difference between the two is that forensic genealogists must meet genealogical proof standards so that their results may be used by the legal system.[39]

This final statement is a misinterpretation of the work of any genealogist who has ethics, knowledge, skill, experience and professional credentials. Whether in legal matters or in reporting on family history research, a practitioner must always differentiate between possibility, probability and proven fact, providing supporting evidence. Anything short of that is not professional.

'Forensic' is one of those words whose meaning has evolved and migrated in recent decades. It was defined generally in the 1970s as to do with use in a court of law. Now it has the additional, and sometimes more prominent, meaning of relating to the application of scientific methods to legal problems or investigation of crime. Fitzpatrick's coining of the phrase 'forensic genealogy' may have been influenced by her scientific background but, as she acknowledged in 2016, conventional genealogy and 'forensic genealogy' employ the same resources and techniques. What she coined was merely a new name for a long established application of genealogical research which, again, she acknowledged. Her term 'forensic genealogy' simply defines the work of a legal genealogist.

It must be said that back in 2012, in her blog *The Demanding Genealogist*, Barbara Jean Mathews stated that Fitzpatrick 'was not narrowly discussing probate work when she coined the term'. She added that when Sharon Sergeant 'broke a few fraud cases involving the publishing industry, she was being a forensic

---

[39] 'I never became a genealogist – I was born a genealogist', interview with Alan Jakman, *More Maiorum*, 45 (2016/10), 14-19, www.moremaiorum.pl/2016-2, accessed 18 July 2018, reprinted in *Forensic Magazine*, www.forensicmag.com/article/2016/12/forensic-genealogy-real-story, accessed 18 July 2018.

genealogist'. Sergeant is known for exposing fraudulent Holocaust memoirs that exploit human tragedy. This certainly is not probate work but it does have legal implications.[40]

In some explanations of 'forensic genealogy' that I have encountered there are suggestions that it goes beyond genealogical (or even legal genealogical) research in that it often involves unconventional sources. If this is the case, one might fairly ask whether certain aspects of forensic genealogy are in any way genealogical? Perhaps if this specialty involves more than legal genealogy it would be more accurately called 'genealogical and forensic research'.

For those outside North America forensic genealogy is unfamiliar and not immediately recognisable as referring to the specialty of legal genealogy, if it can be said to do so. Complexity was added when an organisation was formed, reducing the application of the term. On 19 July 2011 a new 'business league with a professional membership', chartered the previous May in Texas, was announced. This was the Council for the Advancement of Forensic Genealogy (CAFG). The members of its Board of Directors were Leslie Brinkley Lawson (President), Michael S. Ramage (Vice President), Dee Dee King (Secretary and Treasurer), Catherine Desmarais and Kelvin L. Meyers.[41]

In the first issue of its newsletter, *Forensic Genealogy News*, it stated that it had its genesis in 2007 'when a small group of forensic genealogists collaborated in filling the gap that other genealogical groups did not meet in this relatively new field'. It added:

> At that time there were no accepted definitions for heir searcher and forensic genealogist nor was it widely known what the differences between the two were.[42]

That is an odd assertion, given that the term 'heir searcher' has long been widely known and understood in genealogical circles, though 'legal genealogist' is more descriptive. Fitzpatrick's coined term 'forensic genealogist' is but a new name for the same long-established occupation.

Until relatively recently CAFG's website had the following definition:

> *Forensic Genealogy is genealogical research with legal implications, usually involving living people.*
>
> *Using methodology and ethics consistent with the highest standards of the profession,*

---

[40] Mathews, "A Response to 'What Is Forensic Genealogy?'"; Caleb Daniloff, 'Untrue Stories', *Bostonia* (Summer 2009), www.bu.edu/bostonia/summer09/hoax, accessed 18 July 2018.

[41] *Forensic Genealogy News*, 1/1 (July 2011), 1, www.forensicgenealogists.org/wp-content/uploads/CAFG_Vol_1_Issue_1.pdf, accessed 18 July 2018.

[42] *Forensic Genealogy News*, 1/1 (July 2011), 1.

Forensic Genealogy is conducted by unbiased, disinterested third party practitioners with no personal or professional stake in the outcome. … Member forensic genealogists do not work on 'spec' (speculation) or a contingency basis of proceeds paid to clients or beneficiaries. They do not 'recruit' beneficiaries or heirs for their own business, for other firms, or for attorneys. … An 'heir-searcher' is one hired by, or an agent for, individuals or groups to pursue their rights and interests in a court of law, and usually receives payment based on a percentage of the amount recovered for the individual or groups.[43]

Fitzpatrick's definition of 'forensic genealogist' is narrowed by exclusion of the traditional legal genealogist, without whose speculative research many heirs would never discover their unknown inheritance. The CAFG definition above is unfair and unflattering to heir searchers, to say the least.

In 2011 CAFG began its Mentor Program 'for experienced professional genealogists with introductory experience in forensic work and a commitment to building forensic genealogy as a field of concentration'. They were to have support from mentors and access to CAFG resources.[44] In 2012 CAFG extended membership to those enrolled in the Mentor Program, who were to be termed Apprentices (later called Associate Members). Apprentices were to progress to Junior Member and beyond that to Senior Member level (later called Advanced Member).[45]

In June 2014 the membership requirements changed, with the three levels, Associate, Junior and Advanced, replaced by Level I (the new entry level) and Levels II, III and IV. Early in 2018 the membership requirements and levels were revised again. Levels I, II, III and IV became Peer Mentor Program (the entry level), Associate, Junior and Senior. The membership system is rather complex but all four levels of membership have requirements beyond simply paying a fee and promising to abide by its Standards of Practice and Conduct. Having attained what is now Senior level (formerly Level IV) a member is eligible to apply for an accreditation called ForensicGenealogistCredentialed (FGC).[46] In March 2015 CAFG awarded the first two FGC designations to Leslie Brinkley Lawson and

[43] CAFG, 'Hire a Pro', www.forensicgenealogists.org/hire-a-pro, accessed 6 June 2017 [no longer on page].

[44] *Forensic Genealogy News*, 1/2 (Dec. 2011), 1, www.forensicgenealogists.org/wp-content/uploads/CAFG_Vol_1_Issue_2.pdf, accessed 18 July 2018.

[45] *Forensic Genealogy News*, 2/3 (July 2012), 4, www.forensicgenealogists.org/wp-content/uploads/CAFG_Vol_2_Issue_3.pdf, accessed 18 July 2018.

[46] CAFG, 'Membership Levels', www.forensicgenealogists.org/join/membership-levels, accessed 6 June 2017 [page no longer active]; Forensic Genealogy News, 7/1 (Spring 2018), 2, http://www.forensicgenealogists.org/wp-content/uploads/CAFG_Vol_7_Issue_1.pdf, page 2, accessed 18 July 2018; CAFG, 'Credential', www.forensicgenealogists.org/credential, accessed 18 July 2018.

Wanda I. Smith.[47] As of May 2018 no other recipients of this credential have been announced. However, in March 2018 it was announced that Dee Dee King was the first recipient of the organisation's fellowship, 'awarded for a member's outstanding contribution to CAFG and forensic genealogy'.[48]

NON-ACCREDITING SUPPORT / NETWORKING GROUPS

It is perhaps significant that the two US-based accrediting bodies, BCG and ICAPGen, are examining boards, providing credentials for professional genealogists. The organisations in the British Isles and Australasia admit the successful applicant to membership. It may seem that there is little distinction between being granted credentials and being admitted to membership, but the sense of belonging to an organisation may make a difference. Another important factor is that members ordinarily have control over an organisation, while an accrediting body may be a remote wielder of power.

The Genealogical Society of Utah controlled the licensing of Accredited Genealogist (AG) status until 2000, when authority passed to the newly established International Commission for the Accreditation of Professional Genealogists (ICAPGen). Since then AG professionals have elected their commissioners. Similarly, the Board for Certification of Genealogists was initially controlled by appointed trustees. Their number was replenished through election by current trustees. In 2000 the system changed, so that all certified individuals now vote for the trustees.

It would appear that American professional genealogists were lacking a sense of belonging to, or gaining support from, either of the two US-based accrediting bodies back in the 1970s. There seems no other reason why a separate, non-accrediting, organisation was established in the USA. In 1979 a group of genealogists based in Salt Lake City formed the Association of Professional Genealogists (APG).[49] This was a membership organisation formed to provide professionals with a means of sharing expertise, opinions and concerns, and offering mutual support.

It soon grew in popularity. Its 1990 *Directory of Professional Genealogists* listed

---

[47] *Forensic Genealogy News*, 5/2 (March/April 2015), 1, www.forensicgenealogists.org/wp-content/uploads/CAFG_Vol-5_Issue-2_March-April.pdf, accessed 18 July 2018.

[48] *Forensic Genealogy News*, 7/1 (Spring 2018), 1, http://www.forensicgenealogists.org/wp-content/uploads/CAFG_Vol_7_Issue_1.pdf, accessed 9 July 2018; CAFG, 'Fellow Award Announcement', posted 31 March 2018, www.forensicgenealogists.org/awards/fellow-award-announcement, accessed 18 July 2018.

[49] APG, 'History', www.apgen.org/history/index.html, accessed 18 July 2018.

over 500 members resident throughout the USA, as well as nine resident in Canada and 26 outside North America, dispersed between Australia, England, Germany, Israel, New Zealand, Sweden and Switzerland. As of December 2015 APG claimed to represent more than 2,700 genealogists and related professionals throughout the 50 states of the USA as well as Canada and 30 other countries. As of February 2017 the number of members was stated as nearly 2,800.[50]

APG is by far the largest organisation in professional genealogy but there are several other support / networking groups, some covering geographical areas and some not specifically designed for professionals. In May 1987 the Council of Genealogy Columnists was formed at a meeting in Raleigh, North Carolina, during the NGS Conference in the States. In May 2000 it adopted its current name of International Society of Family History Writers and Editors (ISFHWE).[51] Its membership remains primarily within the USA but it is open to all amateur or professional writers on the subject.

Another of the more prominent support / networking groups is the Genealogical Speakers Guild. It was founded in August 1991 at the conclusion of the Federation of Genealogical Societies (FGS) Conference in Fort Wayne, Indiana, by a group of 24 prominent genealogical lecturers.[52] As with ISFHWE, the Guild's membership remains primarily within the USA but it is open to all amateur or professional lecturers on the subject.

Another organisation not confined to professionals is the International Society of Genetic Genealogy (ISOGG). It was formed in 2005 and it provides support and information for anyone interested in the genetic aspect of genealogy, whether they are coming to the subject as absolute beginners or as experts in the field. Membership is free.[53]

The Professional Jewish Genealogists Group is an informal organisation, primarily for networking, so it does not promote itself to the general public. Its members meet annually at the conference of the International Association of Jewish Genealogical Societies. Those interested in getting involved may do so through the conference.

No doubt there are small support / networking groups in various locations.

[50] APG press release, 22 Dec. 2015, www.apgen.org/publications/press/20155editor.htm, accessed 9 July 2018; APG, 'About Us', www.apgen.org/about/index.html, accessed 17 February 2017.
[51] ISFHWE, 'About Us', www.isfhwe.org/home/about-isfhwe, accessed 18 July 2018.
[52] Sharon DeBartolo Carmack, 'Historically Speaking: A look back at the Guild's founding', originally published in *Speak!*, 10 (2011), 11-14, www.genealogicalspeakersguild.org/article.php, accessed 18 July 2018.
[53] ISOGG, 'Welcome to ISOGG', http://isogg.org, accessed 18 July 2018.

For example, Northern Ireland has two, the Association of Ulster Genealogists and Record Agents, and the Society of Genealogists Northern Ireland.

As it currently is a non-accrediting body, *Verband deutschsprachiger Berufsgenealogen* (the Association of German-Speaking Professional Genealogists) could be classed as another support / networking organisation. As already mentioned, it represents the interests of genealogists working in areas in which German is, or has been, spoken. There are requirements for those applying for membership other than simply payment of a fee. The association may become an accrediting body in the future.

Genealogy, Academia and Education

GENEALOGY AND ACADEMIA

In the early years of my career in genealogy I was aware of a slight condescension from certain academic historians, as well as some archivists and librarians, towards ancestral research. It seemed that it was viewed by them as an aimless rummaging through records for scraps of information that had no worth in comparison with *actual* historical research.

Perhaps they saw ancestral research as having little or no structure: no discipline. Perhaps it was that the explosion of interest caused by the publication of Alex Haley's *Roots* had brought masses of ill-prepared hobbyists into record repositories. I cannot judge the legendary impact of the book and the television series in the mid-1970s. In the few years before *Roots* I was an ill-prepared hobbyist. I came to professional research not long after the *Roots* explosion. To what extent it actually impacted on record repositories I cannot say. What is certain is that Alex Haley's novel brought about a new enthusiasm for family history across the globe.

Since the 1970s genealogy's relationship with academia worldwide has been less than positive, but there are signs of great improvement. According to Elizabeth

Shown Mills, a particularly influential figure in American genealogy, the uneasy relationship pre-dates *Roots* by about a century in the USA. She suggests that in the 1870s a new generation of historians, having acquired academic degrees abroad, turned their backs on the traditional practices of American historians, seeing their work as unscientific and egotistical. Along with traditional history, genealogy and local history were dismissed as unworthy of consideration.[54]

Mills suggests that American genealogy itself was partly to blame for its dismissal by the new academic historians. This was because of the espousal of notions of ancestral greatness as well as a long flirtation with eugenics, a pseudo-science concerning race that reached its horrific conclusion in the actions of Adolf Hitler.[55]

It has to be said that genealogy always has had those who might take poetic licence in linking themselves or their patrons to mythical ancestors. The early generations of most ancient Gaelic pedigrees were works of art rather than scientific research. These were created by genealogist-historians for patrons needing impressive bloodlines for political purposes.[56] Similarly, Burkes, the well-known publishing house specialising in the genealogies of the British aristocracy and gentry, in its early days, was content to accept fantasy prequels to many families' actual pedigrees. These practices belong in the past and they should not be visited on genealogists of the twentieth and twenty-first centuries.

While remembering the skeletons in genealogy's cupboard it might be worthwhile to note also that from the nineteenth century forward there has been a growing body of thoroughly researched and properly sourced scholarly articles published by genealogists in the journals of historical and genealogical societies, that has contributed to the collective knowledge of the past.

The idea that genealogists should exercise diligence and judgement in their research and in drawing conclusions was not invented with the introduction of accreditation for professionals in the 1960s. In the nineteenth century people like John Gough Nichols contributed to the fostering of the serious study of genealogy. In the early twentieth century Donald Lines Jacobus very much led the way in America. In the latter half of that century influential genealogists in

---

[54] Elizabeth Shown Mills, 'Genealogy in the "Information Age": History's New Frontier?', *National Genealogical Society Quarterly*: Centennial Issue, 91 (Dec. 2003), 262, www.ngsgenealogy.org/galleries/Ref_Researching/NGSQVol91Pg26077GenealogyHistory.pdf, accessed 18 July 2018.

[55] Mills, 'Genealogy in the "Information Age"', 263-264.

[56] Fergus Gillespie, 'Irish Genealogy and Pseudo-Genealogy', in M.D. Evans and Eileen Ó Dúill, eds., *Aspects of Irish Genealogy: Proceedings of the 1st Irish Genealogical Congress* (Dublin, n.d. [1992]), 123-137.

America pursued the aspiration of proving to academia that genealogy was a discipline worthy of respect.

In 1960, when the American Society of Genealogists published its handbook *Genealogical Research: Methods and Sources*, one of the chapters was 'The Rules of Evidence: A Standard for Proving Pedigrees' by Noel C. Stevenson (1907-1991). Stevenson was a lawyer by profession and he was admitted as a Fellow of the ASG in 1952. In the chapter he stated:

Considerable confusion can be eliminated if everyone engaged in genealogical research followed one body of rules in accepting or rejecting genealogical facts. The advantages are two-fold: (1) Genealogists will compile more accurate pedigrees because it will be necessary for them to apply strict rules in evaluating source material; (2) by applying a recognized standard of proof, it will be possible to assign logical and objective reasons for the acceptance or rejection of genealogical facts, instead of one's own personal rules.

Stevenson suggested that the rules of evidence applied in a court of law in relation to genealogical matters could be applicable to genealogy in general. He asserted that in civil matters in a US court a case was required to be proven by a 'preponderance of the evidence'. This meant that it did not need to be an absolute certainty (as such certainty was rarely provable) but it must offer such evidence 'as to convince the court or jury that the party producing the proof is right'. He distinguished between evidence and proof, stating:

Evidence is the information received, whereas proof is the effect produced by this information. When sufficient evidence is presented, proof is established.

Before going into further detail on the nature and forms of evidence, he suggests:

A genealogist is performing the functions of a court or jury when he sits in judgment on the evidence to prove specific genealogical facts.

Later Stevenson expanded on what he regarded as necessary rules for evaluating evidence in his book *Genealogical Evidence: A Guide to the Standard of Proof Relating to Pedigrees, Ancestry, Heirship, and Family History* (Laguna Hills, California, 1979). His introduction of the phrase 'preponderance of the evidence' had a significant influence on American genealogists and the term found its way into the application requirements of the Board for Certification of Genealogists. However, the legal term was seen as not quite applicable to genealogy so it was modified to create a higher standard. This led to some confusion between the use of the phrase in its legal and its genealogical forms. In 1997 the term was abandoned by BCG but its principles were retained in a modified form of wording.

The new wording was given a new name: the Genealogical Proof Standard (GPS).[57] The GPS is also used by the other US accrediting organisation, ICAPGen, and is in general circulation within the USA.[58]

Another development among American genealogists may lead to confusion for historians and for genealogists in other parts of the world. This is the use of 'three sets of criteria by which sources and their information are classed'. The first is *original* verses *derivative* sources. The second is *primary* verses *secondary* information. The third is *direct* verses *indirect* evidence.[59] What is particularly confusing is that the first (*original* verses *derivative*) is more or less identical to the more widely understood primary verses secondary source, while second set of criteria (*primary* verses *secondary* information) uses the same words for a dissection of the first set of criteria.

Many will see the development of such arcane definitions as important to the advancement of genealogy to a higher level that will impress the academic world; others may regard it as an unnecessary complication.

There are several well-known American books on the subjects of professionalism, evidence and citation. Elizabeth Shown Mills wrote *Evidence! Citation & Analysis for the Family Historian*, published in 1997, and *Evidence Explained: Citing History Sources from Artifacts to Cyberspace*, first published in 2007.

Mills also edited *Professional Genealogy: a Manual for Researchers, Writers, Editors, Lecturers and Librarians*, which appeared in 2001. Known familiarly as *ProGen* (now *ProGen I*) this particular compilation has been used as the textbook for aspiring genealogists in ProGen Study Groups in the USA, each of which is mentored by an Accredited Genealogist or a Certified Genealogist.[60] A new version of *ProGen*, also edited by Mills, appeared in 2018 under the title *Professional Genealogy: Preparation, Practice & Standards*.

While both *ProGen I* and *ProGen PPS* mainly address practices in the USA, both contain valuable guidance for all practitioners. There is much timeless wisdom imparted in *ProGen I*, while *ProGen PPS* has up to date information as well as new topics, such as 'Genetics for Genealogy' by Blaine T. Bettinger and Judy

---

[57] Donn Devine, 'Evidence Analysis', in Elizabeth Shown Mills ed., Professional Genealogy: *a Manual for Researchers, Writers, Editors, Lecturers and Librarians* (Baltimore, 2001), 330-1; Helen F.M. Leary, 'Skillbuilding: Evidence Revisited: DNA, POE, and GPS', originally published in OnBoard 4 (January 1998), https://bcgcertification.org/skillbuilding-evidence-revisited-dna-poe-and-gps, accessed 18 July 2018.

[58] ICAPGen, 'FAQs', www.icapgen.org/faqs, accessed 18 July 2018.

[59] Devine, 'Evidence Analysis', 332-3.

[60] ProGen Study Groups, home page, http://progenstudy.org, accessed 18 July 2018.

G. Russell. *ProGen PPS* has many sections that contain sound advice and useful information for genealogists everywhere. These include Russell's 'Copyright & Fair Use', Melinde Lutz Byrne's 'Educational Preparation', Michael G. Hait's 'Auxiliary Careers' and 'Marketing', Michael S. Ramage's 'Ethical Considerations' and Thomas W. Jones' 'Reasoning from Evidence'.

In 2000 the *BCG Genealogical Standards Manual* was published. A revised edition entitled *Genealogy Standards* was released by BCG in 2014. In 2012 ICAPGen published its *Becoming an Excellent Genealogist: Essays on Professional Research Skills*, edited by Kory L. Meyerink. Tristan L. Tolman & Linda K. Gulbrandsen. The National Genealogical Society, in its Special Topics Series, released *Mastering Genealogical Proof* by Thomas W. Jones in 2013.

It should be stressed that the phrases 'preponderance of the evidence' and Genealogical Proof Standard are not universally known in genealogy throughout the world. These, and the books dealing with citation referred to above, are very much associated with American genealogy. They will not necessarily be encountered by genealogists from other geographical regions except those seeking credentials from BCG or ICAPGen. In those areas of the globe where British English holds sway, for guidance on citation, genealogists should find answers to all problems in the *New Oxford Style Manual* (Oxford, 2016), which incorporates *New Hart's Rules* and *New Oxford Dictionary for Writers and Editors*, both first published in 2005. Another option is *Referencing for Genealogists* by Ian G. Macdonald, published in 2018.

The Genealogical Proof Standard is elevated to the status of a universally held belief in the USA. It may seem like heresy to an American genealogist to question its purpose or value. An over-arching formula for evidence and proof is not necessarily practicable, though the GPS seems to be an indispensable part of the fabric of ancestral research in the USA now. In other regions the only arbiter of evidence and proof in general use might be termed, in simple terms, common sense. By common sense what I mean is evaluation based on a loose and uncodified set of rules, combined with experience. This is not very far removed from Noel C. Stevenson's words, already quoted:

A genealogist is performing the functions of a court or jury when he sits in judgment on the evidence to prove specific genealogical facts.

In reporting their judgement, all genealogists must present the evidence and explain their interpretation in any situation where doubt may arise. The genealogist's responsibility is to differentiate between proven fact, probability and possibility. This should be enough to allow the discerning reader evaluate the genealogist's deductions.

Yes, of course, there is an element of doubt about every 'fact' you may encounter in life. In Irish genealogy you learn from experience that the registered day of birth is not necessarily a 'fact' when you encounter cases of children being baptised a week before their alleged birth date. The 'fact' is that the birth record gave that particular date. When the child was actually born is a matter for conjecture. Similarly, you learn that the informant on a birth record who signed with an 'X' was not necessarily illiterate when you find that they signed a census return as head of household. Of greater consequence, DNA testing may disprove a particular line of paternity, nicely documented and long accepted as correct.

The GPS does not eliminate such eventualities: it elaborates on the differences between proven fact, probability and possibility. In essence the GPS is common sense with an academic-looking makeover. GPS non-believers may view the heavy emphasis on this element of genealogical research as counter-productive navel-gazing. I do not wish to sound flippant about a code in which so many genealogists invest so much of their energy. I was not raised on the GPS or even the 'preponderance of the evidence'. These were not phrases that impacted on my formation as a genealogist, but I feel something like the 'preponderance of the evidence' was always obvious to me. Perhaps instead it was gained through knowledge and experience, but it may in some part have been instinctive.

I cannot vouch for other languages, but English is sophisticated enough to communicate shades of certainty or doubt. Phrases such as 'without doubt', 'almost certainly', 'quite probably', 'uncertain', 'highly unlikely' and 'most improbable' all express different degrees of possibility. A professional genealogist or a seasoned amateur should possess the instinct, knowledge and experience to be able to differentiate between proven fact, probability and possibility, and to be able to clearly communicate the evidence and conclusions. Having said that, perhaps the real strength of the GPS is in making the novice question what they might otherwise accept as a certainty. However, it would appear that the main aim of the GPS's promotion is part of the general codification of genealogical research in order to gain respect from academia. Somehow I do not believe that instinct, knowledge, experience and judgement can be codified and constrained by a set of rules and procedures.

EDUCATIONAL DEVELOPMENTS

Practical experience and exposure to others' comments are the best ways, ultimately, of gaining a real understanding of what is expected in terms of methodology and interpretation of results. Having a mentor can be an important part of learning. However, with so many people developing an interest in the subject in the latter half of the twentieth century, direct mentoring became the privilege of the very few. Other forms of instruction became necessary.

As has been noted already, in 1950 the American Society of Genealogists was involved in starting an annual week-long intensive course on US federal records for experienced researchers, held in Washington, DC. This was the National Institute on Genealogical Research. It continues today, but in December 2015 it was renamed Gen-Fed (Genealogical Institute on Federal Records). There are now several such week-long courses or seminars. Since 1996 the ASG has offered an annual scholarship which allows the recipient to attend one of these courses or 'institutes' as they are called in America. Currently, the recipient of the scholarship may choose one of six courses. These are, along with Gen-Fed; the online Genealogical Research Certificate Program from Boston University; the Genealogical Research Institute of Pittsburgh; the Institute of Genealogy and Historical Research (held at Samford University, Alabama, until 2016, but from 2017 in Athens, Georgia, under the aegis of the Georgia Genealogical Society); the Salt Lake Institute of Genealogy; and GENE 350 (Advanced Genealogical Research) or GENE 201 (Introduction to Genetic Genealogy) from Excelsior College, Albany, New York. Apart from the Boston University and Excelsior College courses, all are week-long 'institutes'.

More comprehensive courses have been available also for many years. In 1961 the Institute of Heraldic and Genealogical Studies was founded by Cecil Humphery-Smith in Canterbury in England. Not to be confused with the week-long courses in America, this independent organisation, run in tandem with a commercial research company, is an institute in the traditional sense. It runs correspondence and residential courses, as well as offering certificates and diplomas.

In 1974 the Society of Australian Genealogists in Sydney began its Diploma in Family Historical Studies (DipFHS) to provide a qualification for genealogists, and places were restricted to members of the society. In 2010 it added an 18-month Certificate in Genealogical Research. This certificate must be obtained before progressing to the diploma course. A Diploma in Family History was offered for many years by GRINZ, the Genealogical Research Institute of New Zealand, but this organisation ceased to exist in 2001. In 1989 University College Dublin, with Sean Murphy as lecturer, was the first Irish third-level institution to introduce a certificate or diploma course in genealogy. It became popular and highly regarded, and for years was the only genealogical course in Ireland offering academic credit. Sadly, the last credit course concluded in 2017.

Brigham Young University in Provo, Utah, was the first institution to offer a four-year bachelor's degree in family history, apparently in 1966.[61] In 1999 the Canadian genealogist Louise St Denis, in partnership with the University of Toronto, began an online certificate course in genealogy. Since then the National Institute for Genealogical Studies has grown. It now offers a range of educational options, from month-long, non-credit courses to credit courses leading to one of eight programmes awarding a Professional Learning Certificate in Genealogical Studies (PLCGS).

The trail-blazers in short events, correspondence and residential courses, certificates, diplomas and online programmes have been joined in the field in more recent years by a plethora of new education providers. While there is a general claim of providing excellence in education, anecdotal evidence suggests that standards are by no means uniform, nor universally impressive.

WHAT IS 'PROFESSIONAL'?

Imbibing knowledge can be done in various ways. Completing a course (with or without a certificate / diploma or academic credit) is a good way of getting a foundation in genealogy. There are alternative ways of getting such a foundation, and they are equally valid. The aspiring genealogist must build on that foundation by acquiring knowledge by experience in conducting research. That is something a course, book, article or consultation cannot teach a student. For a professional genealogist, experience is essential. The word 'professional' has a number of connotations. It may indicate competence. It may indicate belonging to a profession. It may indicate a paid occupation. When applied to genealogy it *should* indicate all three.

Belonging to a profession is a concept that has lost some of its meaning in

---

[61] Claire Mire Bettag, 'Educational Preparation', in Mills, *Professional Genealogy* (2001), 22; Thomas W. Jones, 'Defining Professionalism', in Elizabeth Shown Mills ed., *Professional Genealogy: Preparation, Practice & Standards* (Baltimore, 2018), 38.

recent decades. Nowadays people often use the words 'trade', 'occupation' and 'profession' interchangeably. But traditionally a trade was an occupation that involved manual skills or commerce, while a profession was an occupation that involved some advanced learning. Entering a trade was through apprenticeship. Entering a profession was through academic instruction or apprenticeship or both. In the British Isles until comparatively recent times, solicitors, pharmacists, nurses and journalists, for example, acquired most of their expertise 'on the job'. In the old fashioned sense, the work of a genealogist is a profession, and a genealogist may acquire expertise through academic instruction or 'apprenticeship' or both. However, as with all professions, learning only has real impact when it is matched with practical experience.

The meaning of the word 'professional' that most clearly separates the professional genealogist from the amateur is that of paid occupation. Ancestral research is a field of study unlike most others in that it may be a popular hobby or an area of advanced learning, or both. Few other hobbies have the same blurred line between amateur and professional. Deltiologists collect postcards as a hobby, while postcard dealers sell them. Bibliophiles collect books as a hobby, while book dealers sell them. There is no need to add the word 'professional' to distinguish a postcard dealer or book dealer from his customer. On the other hand, numismatists collect and study coins and philatelists collect and study postage stamps, and you find the word 'professional' used in conjunction with numismatist or philatelist to describe coin and stamp dealers. Professional genealogists do not *deal* in pedigrees in the same sense, but they have a paid occupation in a field that for most is a hobby.

I have used the word 'hobbyists' already in referring to the majority of those undertaking family history. That may sound disrespectful but it most accurately describes those pursuing genealogical research as a hobby. What other word might do instead? The reason for using it in the first place was that, in the context of genealogy, certain people mistakenly interpret 'amateur' as a pejorative term. Having used 'hobbyist' already I may go as far as to say it is pejorative if applied to more experienced and knowledgeable amateurs.

In an entirely different sphere, Bobby Jones was one of the greatest golfers of all time and he was an amateur, meaning that he did not play golf as a paid occupation, but he was not a hobbyist golfer. In the sense of hobby / profession, golf is analogous to genealogy. In both pursuits there are highly regarded and skilful amateurs who choose, for varying reasons, to remain as what golfers now call 'career amateurs'. On the other hand, there are those who decide to make it their occupation.

There are legions of 'career amateur' genealogists who have contributed enormously to the discipline of genealogy. The vast majority of people in ancestral research for the long haul are amateur in that sense. Genealogical societies, some of them dating from as early as the mid-nineteenth century, were founded and nurtured mainly by amateurs. As already noted, many of these societies have been producing learned journals for decades, setting standards for the writing of family histories and adding to the body of reference material for all. Indeed, many who evolved into professional genealogists started their careers as members of such societies and continued to contribute to the excellent work of those organisations while pursuing their professional careers.

A BROAD CHURCH

Along with professionals, 'career amateur' genealogists have a desire to sharpen their skills and expand their knowledge. Hobbyists who wish to go further in genealogy also have a need for learning. The introduction of certificate, diploma and post-graduate courses in genealogy and related fields is something to be welcomed in that it provides guidance for a greater number of people than one-to-one mentoring can offer. However, there is a danger that too much emphasis on attaining such qualifications may lead to undervaluing other routes to knowledge that have long been available in genealogy.

Unlike many other areas of learning, genealogy has always been a broad church. It accommodates everyone from the absolute beginner to the confident hobbyist or aspirant professional to the expert 'career amateur' or accredited professional. In seeking to gain respect for genealogy from academia there is a danger that some valid routes to knowledge may be closed off. Perhaps academia's attitudes are different in various regions. In my part of the world most academic historians, archivists and librarians have now learned enough about genealogy to understand that it is indeed a broad church: that there are experts and beginners, and the whole spectrum in between. The accredited professional or career amateur is not confused with the absolute beginner. All are treated with respect, but there is not an assumption that all people doing ancestral research are unfamiliar with the use of records.

It is interesting to note that as long ago as the mid-1980s an Australian academic historian, writing a guide-book on ancestral research, made a very insightful observation. Now retired from her university career, Noeline Kyle has published several biographies and books on the subject of women's history, as well as guidance on writing family history. In 1985 her *Tracing Family History in Australia* was published. In it she observed that in the course of their research family historians use 'more primary sources than many good BA Honours history students do in rigorous university courses'.[62]

That is very believable. A report published in 1993 by a group of organisations representing American historians and archivists, quoted by Elizabeth Shown Mills, stated that 'most graduate students acquire archival research skills – to the extent they do acquire these skills – not as a part of graduate training but through time consuming and expensive exercises in trial and error'.[63]

In Ireland history students (undergraduate or post-graduate) appear to have relatively little exposure to manuscripts compared to genealogists (amateur or professional). It is likely that when history students venture into primary sources they do so with as much trepidation as the average novice family historian. It is only by gaining familiarity with the records that an appreciation of their context and scope is acquired.

I have long thought of the prejudice of some (and it was only some) historians, archivists and librarians towards genealogy as little more than academic snobbery, and perhaps a lack of understanding of the methods and approach of true genealogists. Times have changed. In my sphere, if any prejudice or lack of understanding remains it is miniscule. However, as recently as 2003 Elizabeth Shown Mills was much exercised about the continuing problem of lack of academic respect and recognition for genealogists: 'Are we content for other disciplines to dismiss genealogy as an "ego trip" – History Lite? Will we accept a role some others propose for us – that of Data Sweeper, mere drudge labor to boost the productivity of "real" historians?'[64]

In that same 2003 article Mills made a very good suggestion as to how academic historians might be enlightened about standards and methods employed by genealogists. She proposed that scholarships be made available to post-graduate history students for attending genealogical 'institutes' and major conferences. This could 'build vital bridges between our branch of history and

---

[62] Noeline Kyle, *Tracing Family History in Australia* (North Ryde, NSW, 1985), 139, quoted in Faye M. Young, 'The Role of the Professional Genealogist in Australia', in Geoffrey Burkhardt and Peter Procter, eds., *Bridging the Generations: Fourth Australasian Congress on Genealogy and Heraldry, Canberra 1986* (Canberra, 1986), 435.

[63] Mills, 'Genealogy in the "Information Age"', 275.

[64] Mills, 'Genealogy in the "Information Age"', 261.

tomorrow's academic historians.[65] It would be far better to demonstrate to academia that genealogy is a serious study than to change the nature of genealogy in the hope of admission through a door it has no need to enter.

BARRIER-BUILDING

Fifteen years on from the 2003 article by Mills, is genealogy still the subject of academic snobbery in the USA? Does genealogy have an inferiority complex when it comes to measuring up against academia? Are some of the newer certificate or diploma courses designed to provide academic status rather than impart knowledge? Does the Genealogical Proof Standard make better genealogists or make their practices seem more academically acceptable? These are not just random questions. Now more than ever, there are definite moves within elements of genealogy towards 'raising standards' and 'qualifications', as if higher and higher academic hurdles were needed to make the study of ancestral research complete.

The American blogger James Tanner may not have had that exact thought in mind when he wrote an interesting blogpost in 2013 entitled 'The Status of Genealogists' in the Greater Academic Community'.[66] Tanner has decades of experience in law, computers and genealogical research. He teaches genealogy and helps visitors to the Brigham Young University FamilySearch Library in Provo. He also writes the *Genealogy's Star* blog.

In the blogpost he referred to the 2003 article by Elizabeth Shown Mills.[67] In the article she noted changes in attitudes towards genealogical researchers among archivists and librarians, citing genealogy's 'investments in quality and standards' as the cause. She posed the question as to how long it would take for genealogy to gain similar trust from 'the rest of the academic world', including historians and 'educational institutions where we need degree programs in generational history', as she termed serious genealogical research. She drew a distinction between what she termed family tree climbers, traditional genealogists and 'generational historians'.

Mills stated that genealogists had 'created a scholarly field and a profession'. However, she proposed that acceptance of 'generational history'

[65] Mills, 'Genealogy in the "Information Age"', 275.
[66] James Tanner, 'The Status of Genealogists in the Greater Academic Community', *Genealogy's Star*, posted 10 Nov. 2013, http://genealogysstar.blogspot.ie/2013/11/the-status-of-genealogists-in-greater.html, accessed 18 July 2018.
[67] Mills, 'Genealogy in the "Information Age"', 260-277.

by academia required that a genealogist have some formal education in history, have accreditation (as a genealogist) and pursue a degree in 'generational history' (when such becomes available), as well as publishing research results in peer-reviewed journals of an academic standard.

Looking at her proposals a decade later, James Tanner suggested that in seeking such acceptance from academia the 'generational historian' was seeking assimilation into academic history rather than gaining academic acceptance for genealogy. He felt that removing the barrier between academia and 'generational history' would result in placing it instead between 'generational historians' and the rest of the genealogical field.

Tanner observed that 'all professions move towards exclusivity'. He added:

If I produce high academic quality work and it is ignored by the "academic community" solely on the basis that I am a genealogist without academic qualifications, then the loss is to the academic community.

It is a fact that most professions, and even many trades, have replaced their apprenticeship entrance options with exclusively academic ones. Genealogy has not yet entirely succumbed to the notion that academic qualifications are superior to 'on the job' learning. Because of its dual status as a hobby and an occupation, genealogy is a profession with unique characteristics: there are no hobbyist solicitors, pharmacists or nurses. Due to the fact that the initial entry to genealogy is primarily as a hobby, it is entirely appropriate that apprenticeship (or its equivalent) continues to be an option. This in no way diminishes its status as a profession.

One of the reasons Mills proposed the term 'generational historian' is because of the existence of what she termed 'family tree climbers' calling themselves genealogists. I agree with her that new genealogy-enthusiasts should not bandy about the term 'genealogist', or for that matter 'family historian'. Even hobbyists with some mileage on the clock should pause for thought before proclaiming themselves genealogists. When I was first working as a freelance researcher, full-time, for the Genealogical Office in Dublin, learning on the job, I told myself that I would be entitled to call myself a genealogist after three years in that position. No one told me I could do so and no one told me I could not. It did not impact on anyone but me. It was gradually over the years that I grew into being a genealogist.

It seems to be almost universally accepted now that 'genealogist' and 'family historian' are two different things. I never have subscribed to that notion. A genealogist does not merely reconstruct the skeletal remains of the family tree so that the family historian can tell the family's story. A genealogist may attempt to reconstruct any aspect of a family's past. It is regrettable that the word is so narrowly applied nowadays. The 'professional genealogist' may be distinguished from the novice, but what distinguishes the true professional from the self-proclaimed 'professional'? What of the experienced 'career amateur', abandoned in an ocean teeming with beginners? I have no desire to be a 'generational historian'. I am content to be a genealogist, even if people think that means that I collect ancestors as a hobby.

Genealogy is indeed a broad church, ranging from the absolute beginner to the expert. For people on the outside there are few markers to distinguish a genealogist's level of expertise or status. Membership of a prestigious club such as the American Society of Genealogists is one measure. Fellowship of a respected organisation is another. A reputation gained by years of writing, lecturing and conducting research for clients is a less tangible one. A certificate or diploma is a measure of educational achievement. A professional credential is a measure of all-round competence.

Yes, genealogy is an area of historical research but it does not have to conform to narrow academic criteria to prove its validity. As Mills said, genealogists have 'created a scholarly field and a profession', but genealogy is not confined to the professional or scholarly end of things. It is a broad church that can accommodate many ways of acquiring knowledge. Perhaps genealogy needs to start feeling good about its achievements rather than trying to be something else entirely. Genealogy does not need visible barriers or academic approval in order to have worth. If serious genealogists produce 'high academic quality work', as James Tanner suggested, that is all the proof needed.

STANDARDS OR BARRIERS?

In recent years there have been signs of attempts to place barriers between 'generational historians' (or equivalent hierarchies) and the rest of the genealogical field. Perhaps in some cases the primary intent is proving genealogy's worth to some external entity and the barriers are incidental.

In the USA the Council for the Advancement of Forensic Genealogy (CAFG) was formed in 2011. As already mentioned, a few years before, a group of 'forensic genealogists' decided that this 'relatively new field' was not being covered by any existing organisation. The term 'forensic genealogy' as earlier coined by Colleen Fitzpatrick, was applicable to genealogy in relation to legal matters. CAFG reduced the definition to apply only to work undertaken on behalf of courts or government agencies, explicitly ruling the practices of traditional legal genealogists as beyond the pale. This was because these professionals additionally conduct speculative research and may receive payment as a percentage of an heir's inheritance.

The impression given by CAFG's criteria is that the traditional legal genealogist is a pariah. Perhaps the situation is different in the USA: I have no experience of the American system, though I know Irish genealogists who have collaborated with American heir searchers or legal genealogists. Of course, there are individuals of dubious reputation and motives in all areas of genealogy but, on the other hand, many highly respected and expert legal genealogists operate throughout the world and provide a valuable service.

CAFG's exclusion of such practitioners is one aspect of the organisation's policies that is difficult to understand. Another aspect suggests that it aspires to overshadow existing accreditation for professional genealogists. Of course, CAFG accredits only researchers in a certain sector, those who act as 'disinterested third party practitioners with no personal or professional stake in the outcome' of legal matters. Nonetheless, its entry requirements and elaborate hierarchical structure suggest that merely having professional credentials from an established accrediting body is of little value.

The entry level for CAFG membership (which does not merit inclusion in the organisation's online list of members) requires that the applicant have proof of some basic instruction in genealogy. This is quite reasonable and attendance at any two of a variety of short courses and conferences is accepted. Alongside these are alternative entry qualifications. They include having an AG or CG credential, having a degree in genealogy or being recognised by a court or government agency as an expert witness in genealogy. Surely such qualifications should merit more than just admission to the lowest rung of CAFG's ladder!

Indeed, I would suspect that being a genealogist with professional credentials or a recognised expert witness was sufficient for acceptance in legal matters before the advent of an organisation demanding more. After all, legal or forensic genealogy is the application of genealogical research to legal matters: it is not a separate discipline. A genealogist with credentials already possesses the genealogical skills and expertise needed for the specialty. They do not need their credentials as genealogists rubber-stamped by a third party. Of course, extra skills pertaining to the law, such as familiarity with the legal requirements of the various jurisdictions and the ability to present information for or in court, need to be acquired.

No doubt CAFG has honourable motives, but its *modus operandi* smacks of exclusivity, regulation and barriers. Its hierarchical structure, with four levels of membership before reaching the pinnacle of success with the designation of FGC, seems excessive. One might reasonably question the necessity of such a superstructure beyond normal credentials for genealogists. Is it for the good of the genealogist working with legal matters or is it to impress the legal profession?

ACADEMIC BARRIERS

Occasionally people come up with the bright idea that professional genealogy needs regulation. Often these people are not themselves practising professional genealogists. In August 2014 a meeting was held in Glasgow to discuss what *Eastman's Online Genealogy Newsletter* reported as 'the potential need for a framework for genealogical education, licensing, and/or regulation in the British Isles'.[68]

---

[68] Dick Eastman, 'Symposium in Glasgow – The Future of Professional Genealogy', *Eastman's Online Genealogy Newsletter*, posted 30 August 2014, http://blog.eogn.com/2014/08/30/symposium-in-glasgow-the-future-of-professional-genealogy, accessed 18 July 2018.

Eastman's report did not state who had called this meeting, but most of those who addressed the gathering had associations with the genealogy courses run at the University of Strathclyde.

The comments in response to the Eastman article included one from a representative of the Institute of Heraldic and Genealogical Studies in Canterbury. It pointed out that the Institute had been providing courses and qualifications for more than half a century and that it had not been consulted about the meeting nor invited to address it.

Three long-established associations, AGRA, ASGRA and AGI, provide credentials for professional genealogists throughout the British Isles. It is perhaps telling that none of the three accrediting bodies was given an official invitation to the meeting nor was their general membership informed of it in advance. It is true that 'regulation' of genealogy as a profession does not exist in the British Isles, or anywhere else on the planet. Professional credentials are available to those who wish to try to prove their competence. Regulation is an entirely different matter. Regulation in this case means a course of 'genealogical education' that you *must* complete before you can obtain a 'licence' and you *must* have a licence to practise as a genealogist. In other words, a barrier!

Another comment in response to the Eastman article asked the following rhetorical question: 'Is someone who has been making a living from genealogy for thirty years but has no academic qualifications somehow a worse genealogist than someone who has recently completed an academic course?'

This question was answered in a forceful rhetorical answer the following year:

'*"I've been doing this for 20 years", or whatever. So what? You may have been doing it well or badly for 20 years, but how is anyone to judge?*

I've been fixing up old cars for 45 years, and I'm hardly a professional and certainly not a qualified mechanic ...'

These were the words of Bruce Durie in an interview. A transcript of the interview was published in *Eastman's Online Genealogy Newsletter* in June 2015.[69] The interview apparently was linked to a webinar held on 10 June 2015 promoting the development of a 'Register of Qualified Genealogists'. Those listed on the

---

[69] Dick Eastman, 'The Development of a Register of Qualified Genealogists (RQG) Webinar Held on the 10th June', *Eastman's Online Genealogy Newsletter*, posted 16 June 2015, https://blog.eogn.com/2015/06/16/the-development-of-a-register-of-qualified-genealogists-rqg-webinar-held-on-the-10th-june, and appended transcript of interview with Bruce Durie, http://eogn.com/images/newsletter/2015/BD%20Interview%2015%20June%202015.pdf, accessed 18 July 2018.

programme of speakers for the webinar were all associated with the genealogy courses run at Strathclyde.

Durie's interview contained other intemperate, dismissive and derogatory comments about professional genealogy in general, such as:

"Why not just join such-and-such a membership body?"

There are some membership and certification organisations out there who like to pretend they are in some way the "gatekeepers" for the profession. Well, who made them so? No names, but have any of these bodies subjected their certifications, their assessments and their assessors to objective, external, third-party scrutiny or validation? Has any of them been looked at by the NCQF, OFQUAL or the Qualifications and Curriculum Development Agency in England, Wales and Northern Ireland, or the Scottish Qualifications Agency, NARIC and so on? No. Does any of them actually know what level equivalent their certifications are at, compared to, say, the Dundee or Strathclyde or IHGS courses and qualifications? NO. They've just made it up, frankly. And these days, that wouldn't even happen with a Cycling Proficiency Certificate or a Bronze Medal in Lifesaving.

Towards the end of the interview the following questions and answers appeared:

Q. What about all the working genealogists out there who don't have a qualification?

A. Get a qualification! These tend to be the same people who say "I am a Certified This or an Accredited That". And I say, "So how do I become a Certified/Accredited Thing?" And they say: "You have to pass a test". Fine. To be a Qualified Genealogist, you have to pass a test - it's called 'Get A Qualification'. Or, get your certifying/accrediting body to have its tests equivalenced against a proper qualification. And in the meantime, please stop complaining that you can't join one body that has what you perceive as a barrier, while you yourselves put up a barrier to joining, but one that isn't universally recognised.

Q. So, where is this all heading?

A. We are, inevitably, heading for that happy day when genealogy will be a graduate profession, just like Engineering, Nursing, Psychology and Accountancy. It may take a generation, but so what? It took Dentistry a generation, but now, who goes to an unqualified dentist who has "been doing it for 20 years"? There's no point standing on the beach and telling the tide to go back. Frankly, this IS going to happen. Better to learn to swim. And get a proper swimming qualification.

In 2006 Durie became Honorary Editor of the *Irish Genealogist*, the journal of the Irish Genealogical Research Society. In his first issue he introduced himself with a detailed account of the qualifications, achievements and appointments he gained in various fields before deciding to concentrate on writing and developing a career as a genealogist.[70] How much experience of genealogical research he had at that stage was not stated.

He was then 'Academic Director, Genealogical Studies at the University of Strathclyde, Glasgow, where he has established a new set of postgraduate professional qualifications in genealogy, family history and heraldry'. In the interview published by Eastman, Durie commented '... I started them precisely because there was no educational/professional qualifications framework at that time', stating that he no longer was running these courses. However, as late as March 2017, according to his website at that time, he is working with the genealogical course people at Strathclyde in developing a Masters programme.[71]

Though Durie originated the courses at Strathclyde, he does not have what he would describe as a qualification in genealogy. He does, however, have a profile page on the Register of Qualified Genealogists website.[72] This anomaly is explained on the website's FAQ page, where it states that 'creators of courses that enable people to become qualified cannot take the courses themselves to become qualified'[73] That explanation might prompt the rhetorical question: 'You may have had the knowledge and experience to create a course well or badly, but how is anyone to judge?'

The Register of Qualified Genealogists (RQG) was set up eventually in early 2016, with the launch of its website. The website indicates that 'accepted qualifications' are those given by the Institute of Heraldic and Genealogical Studies, the University of Dundee and, of course, the University of Strathclyde. These three are the only institutions that 'currently provide courses assessed to the standard for recognition'. However, the Register does not rule out courses given anywhere in the world 'that may meet the standard and can be considered for recognition'.[74]

In the meantime, those studying towards a qualification from one of the three recognised institutions may obtain student membership of RQG and have a profile of the Register's website.[75] This anomaly too is explained on the website's FAQ page, where it states 'our student members are still on their way to being

[70] 'Appointment of Honorary Editor of *The Irish Genealogist*', *Irish Genealogist*, 12/1 (2006), 6.

[71] Dr Bruce Durie - Genealogist and Heraldist, home page, www.brucedurie.co.uk, accessed 26 March 2017.

[72] RQG, 'Durie, Dr. Bruce', www.qualifiedgenealogists.org/profiles/durie-bruce, accessed 18 July 2018.

[73] RQG, FAQS 'Are all members of RQG qualified?', www.qualifiedgenealogists.org/faqs, accessed 18 July 2018.

[74] RQG, 'Accepted Qualifications', www.qualifiedgenealogists.org/accepted-qualifications, accessed 18 July 2018.

[75] RQG, 'Join', www.qualifiedgenealogists.org/join, accessed 18 July 2018.

qualified – but they have made the commitment'.[76]

While Durie's interview suggests that the Register does not rate the practices of the world's long-established accrediting bodies, two of the three accrediting bodies covering the British Isles have facilitated those completing courses run by the three institutions promoted by the Register. Since June 2013 ASGRA has reduced practical requirements for those having diplomas from Strathclyde, and since April 2015 a similar arrangement exists for those with diplomas from Dundee. Since September 2014 AGRA has reduced practical requirements for those having qualifications from Canterbury or Strathclyde, and since June 2018 has similar arrangements for holders of the advanced certificate from Pharos. Evidently ASGRA and AGRA see some benefit in recognising these qualifications but, of course, both retain the traditional routes to membership as well. Accredited Genealogists Ireland (AGI), the third accrediting body, does not accept completion of courses as part of its accreditation criteria, but does recognise the benefit they may be to applicants in developing their knowledge and skills.

From the perspective of a genealogist rather than someone promoting a course of lectures, I would contend that there is one important difference between holding a certificate or diploma and being accredited as a genealogist. The certificate or diploma shows that the holder has knowledge of genealogy, acquired through academic learning. Accreditation shows that they have both knowledge of genealogy and experience of genealogical research, regardless of how they were acquired. Certificates or diplomas are not a substitute for accreditation: they are a step in the direction of becoming a fully rounded genealogist and gaining professional credentials from an accrediting body.

[76] RQG, 'Are all members of RQG qualified?'.

Question: Does a certificate from a genealogical education program constitute certification? [Answer:] No. In professional fields (as opposed to some technical fields), a certificate or a degree from a college, university, or institute attests only that you have completed certain educational coursework. Certification, which determines whether you have acquired expertise in a field, is a separate matter whose function is performed by boards or bars that are independent of teaching institutions.

- Board for Certification of Genealogists, Frequently Asked Questions: Certification[77]

---

[77] BCG, Frequently Asked Questions, 'Certification', https://bcgcertification.org/process/faq, accessed 18 July 2018.

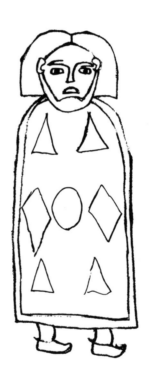

SECTION 3

Developing a Career in Genealogical Research

SHIFTING SANDS

Genealogy was once the preserve of the amateur society that nurtured the hobby, promoted volunteerism and led the way towards scholarly research through publishing journals and organising lectures or conferences. The vast majority of professional genealogists began their careers as 'hobbyists', nurtured in that atmosphere. It was a good introduction to the subject. Amateur societies are still alive and well, but they seem not to be growing apace with family history as a hobby. They no longer are as central to the whole fabric of genealogy.

Technology has changed how people interact with family history. Individuals still join societies, attend lectures, go to conferences and generally rub shoulders with other enthusiasts. But more and more individuals are researching online, conversing with faceless strangers in Internet forums, chatrooms or hangouts, watching webinars and generally ploughing a lone furrow. The budding professional genealogists coming from this background are somewhat at a disadvantage, but generally they remedy this by becoming more involved with like-minded people before venturing into a career.

Before technology held sway, there was no substitute for the hard slog.

Searching through original documents or microfilm copies or index books in libraries and archives was time consuming and often tedious. But being in a place of research had atmospheric charm and, more importantly, it afforded an intimate relationship with the records. Scanning documents of a similar nature over and over with the human eye, turning the pages, seeing names written in different hands and finding nuggets of information gave a familiarity with sources that was immeasurably rewarding for the development of research skills.

Now we have instant results online, with minimal effort. Discovering information in the comfort of our own homes, at any hour of the day or night, has its own charms. However, the intimacy with the source material is lacking in that circumstance. In many cases we cannot *virtually* 'turn the page', so we have to accept that a single, undated, page is what the database says it is. Instead of having a deep understanding of the source, we familiarise ourselves with the differing search facilities of various databases, learn their quirks and slowly become aware of their individual shortcomings. Unless we have prior experience of searching the original sources we are dependent on the sometimes inaccurate background descriptions given on the relevant websites.

In the past, as material was transferred to microfilm the originals usually were removed from public access. Now, as the microfilmed copies are digitised for online consumption the microfilms often are removed from public access. Getting to see original records is a problem for all genealogists and it will only grow as more material is digitised. This process is creating a universal dependency on online versions of records. We have instant access to images of documents but we have less intimacy with those documents. Genealogy has reached a point where access to records is more 'democratic' but is also largely monopolised by giant corporations. Profitability and competition are the main criteria that govern access and the quality of that access. The perceived 'democracy' of this new world of instant online access is attracting a much larger, less discerning audience for genealogy: an audience seduced by television programmes and advertisements that make it seem simple.

The popularity of online family history research appears to grow and grow, while the role of amateur societies appears to weaken. So too does the role of the professional genealogist. As more and more sources go online the notion that genealogy is solely a do-it-yourself thing gathers more credibility. The need for familiarity with the sources and for interpretation of results is appreciated by a smaller proportion of those new to the hobby.

The typical Internet-age beginner may not recognise the need for the professional genealogist at all – everything is online and it is just a matter of using all those databases. I was told as much a few years ago by someone working in the media who dabbled in ancestral research. He was of the opinion that professional genealogists were redundant because online sources were available to all and, apparently, needed no interpretation, no context and no back-ups.

Of course, he was completely wrong, but he and others of a like mind would not recognise the need for interpretation, context and back-ups. To illustrate the point, I will recall an experience I had a while ago in the Genealogy Service at the National Archives in Dublin. I was on duty when someone came in despairing that they could not find a particular family in either the 1901 or the 1911 Census returns for Ireland. They had even spoken to a consultant in another national record repository in Dublin who was baffled by the situation.

The 1901 and 1911 returns had been put online some years ago by the National Archives. Prior to that it was necessary to know where a family lived, to identify the relevant District Electoral Division (DED), to identify the DED number and then order out the relevant microfilm to search through and locate the correct entry. The census returns going online was a major landmark for Irish genealogy. However, the database has its quirks. One of these concerns the transcribers' interpretation of surnames with the prefix 'O', and how the search facility deals with these. "O'Brien", "OBrien" and "O Brien" may turn up different results. In some cases this has been corrected in the search facility, but not in all. Another quirk is that some files and even some entire DEDs were omitted accidentally from the database.

As it turned out, my enquirer was looking for a family whose surname was transcribed peculiarly in 1911 and whose DED was missing in 1901. Familiarity with the original source and with the quirks of the database allowed me quite easily to solve the problem. However, it was so long since I had to use the old finding aids that I had to pause for a moment to recall the exact procedure for ordering out the microfilm of the census. This sort of problem solving is not complicated: it just involves familiarity with the source, and experience.

People brought to ancestral research by television and online resources are at a great disadvantage. Like the media man who told me I was redundant, these people think that it is only a matter of manipulating databases in order to fish out ancestors: that it is a matter of perseverance and luck rather than experience and skill. Sadly, they are encouraged in this belief by some of the online data providers, who urge novices to start constructing family trees before they have even thought about asking basic questions among family members.

As a result of the lure of the new glossy image I would imagine that there are thousands of people around the globe happily digging out information about someone else's ancestors in the mistaken belief that these individuals are their own antecedents. No doubt this was happening before, to an extent, but I would venture that it has become much more widespread in recent years. The sharing of online family trees must account for any number of mistakenly spliced pedigrees, simply because of one or both of the sharers having wrong information. This is a major source of what I call 'genealogical virus'.

So, is there a role for the professional in the future of genealogy? You might think that the professional is an endangered species. I would not argue with that. Conducting genealogical research for a living is a precarious occupation. Enquiries can be unpredictably plentiful or sparse, with no seasonal pattern. The percentage of enquiries that translate to do-able or worthwhile research and then convert into commissions is relatively low. The 'democracy' of online access and the general lack of appreciation of the intricacies of research mean that the increased number of online hobbyists does not guarantee increased business for professional genealogists.

At the same time there has been a population explosion among professional researchers. With well over two thousand people around the globe advertising themselves as genealogists it would make you wonder what is attracting new practitioners and how well equipped they are to take on other people's research. Empirical evidence suggests that a proportion of the new practitioners come from the audience seduced by television programmes and advertisements. To them, genealogy is a growing business and they want to be part of it.

It is interesting that in its annual report for 2015-2016, the *Bureau québécois d'attestation de compétence en généalogie* (BQACG) observed that an increasing weakness was perceptible among candidates for its credentials, in terms of general knowledge of primary research sources and reference books. Some candidates who did well otherwise lost points on basic questions because of their lack of knowledge of the variety of sources, apparently due to over-dependence on computer databases.[78]

There is a huge distinction to be drawn between the new practitioners who

---

[78] FQSG, 'Rapport annuel de la présidente 2015-2016', http://federationgenealogie.qc.ca/federation/rapport-annuel, accessed 10 March 2017 [no longer on page].

come from the seduced audience and the new practitioners who have looked seriously at genealogy and decided to work towards a career in the profession. Nevertheless, the serious practitioner must go beyond computer databases to become familiar with genealogical sources, and to address the client's needs.

Nowadays, while giving advice or assessing research requests, I find myself spending more and more time querying the client about the information they supply. It is unprofessional to take the client's information at face value. 'My tree is online' is not a sufficient answer to the question 'how did you trace back to this ancestor?' Even if the 'tree' has attached sources it does not explain the research process or guarantee that the sources are relevant. It is necessary to establish what the client knew from family information (if anything) and how they progressed from there before contemplating further research options. The initial client reaction to being questioned about the care they have taken involves some degree of irritation, but when the situation is explained they generally appreciate the necessity for the questioning and the conscientiousness.

Thankfully, after being drawn into a labyrinth of records they do not understand, many novices have the common sense to realise that there is more to genealogical research than tapping names into search boxes. Often they conclude that they need to apply 'genealogical anti-virus' to their family tree. At that point they may decide to learn more about the process of genealogical research, about the context of the records they are using, and even about the most effective way of manipulating online databases.

So, what has this got to do with professional genealogists (with or without credentials)?

Professional genealogists, especially enthusiastic new practitioners, are so absorbed in the process of conducting research that they may sometimes lose sight of the clients' requirements. Clients are not a uniform group. They range from the budding hobbyist to the 'career amateur', and even not infrequently the professional. It is worthwhile to pause occasionally and reflect on what each particular client may expect, especially one who has never before engaged a genealogist.

The professional genealogist needs to understand the level of familiarity the potential client has with the process and needs to respond appropriately for that level. The potential client, on the other hand, needs to determine that the professional genealogist they are about to engage is competent and has integrity.

In this time of great change in the development of genealogy all that is certain is that things are changing. In such circumstances it is more important than ever that some stability is maintained. Professional genealogists need to embrace and maintain standards of practice. Adhering to a code of ethics is not the same as maintaining standards of practice. Promising to behave ethically falls far short of guaranteeing knowledge, skill and experience. These qualities are guaranteed by the professional credentials provided by the various accrediting bodies. But the credentials may be acquired only after the practitioner gains experience.

WHY A CAREER IN GENEALOGICAL RESEARCH?

This is a very important question. Before seriously considering such a career any aspiring professional genealogist should seriously consider their motives.

If they think 'genealogy is an expanding market and there is loads of money to be made in it', they should look for a lucrative career in another field. There is no such thing as a rich genealogist, or so the saying goes. Some people make a decent amount of money as ancestral researchers, especially if they conduct probate work. Good business people, who are disciplined about their time and resources, can make a decent living. But the truth is that most people who take up genealogy as a main career have already gained a pension from a former career or have a spouse with a separate income. The big money to be made in genealogy is made by large international corporations on behalf of their investors or shareholders. By all accounts, they do not over-pay their employees. So if your incentive for becoming a professional genealogist is the money you will earn, think again.

If the aspiring professional genealogist is motivated by a passion for the subject, they should have a long hard think about their finances. If they are about to retire (early or not) with a pension and wish to try their hand at pursuing a long-held dream, they probably are in a good position to proceed. However, they should remember that they are entering into a profession, not a paid hobby. They need to think about the financial viability of their venture and do all relevant costings. This is not merely for the benefit of their bank balance, but for the good of genealogical research as a profession.

When I was a novice professional researcher, one of my senior colleagues explained to me why genealogists had to charge such low fees. It was because 'old dears are happy to do research for pin-money'. My colleague herself was nearing the age bracket to which she referred. For those unfamiliar with the term, pin-money was the dress allowance given to women by their husbands. Even by that

SECTION 3 - DEVELOPING A CAREER IN GENEALOGICAL RESEARCH

time it was an archaic expression. A more familiar equivalent would be 'pocket money'. There are still lots of people happy to do research for pocket money. Research is fun! Getting a little money for it makes it more fun! If you are thinking of entering the profession of genealogy, bring your self-respect with you. Make sure the fee you charge covers costs and gives you some earnings. Otherwise you are doing charity work and undermining true professionals who are trying to make a living. How high a fee can you charge? You can charge as much as you like. It is up to your clients to decide whether you are worth it.

MY START IN GENEALOGY

I had a somewhat unusual beginning to my career in genealogical research. I started in 1979 as a member of the freelance research panel of the Genealogical Office (GO), which was Ireland's state-run institution with responsibility for genealogy and heraldry, situated in Dublin Castle. I was a very naïve nineteen year old with a decade of interest in family and local history behind me, but with very little knowledge of practical research or sources beyond those of the General Register Office (civil records of birth, death and marriage). The Genealogical Office took me on as a researcher, not because of my non-existent expertise, but, because I had a passion for the subject.

Over the next few years I was given informal training by GO staff and by my generous elders on the research panel. I often think of my early days in professional genealogy as an apprenticeship. As mentioned already, at the time I set my sights on a three-year period after which I might dare to call myself a genealogist. That 'apprenticeship' was a wonderful introduction to my profession, one I was very fortunate to experience. Sadly, that avenue is no longer open to aspiring professional genealogists in Ireland.

Accreditation or professional credentials were not a big priority with the GO freelance researchers back in 1979. They had the kudos of being attached to the state's genealogical institution and they were not seeking commissions elsewhere. Before family history events were held within Ireland and long before the world dominance of the Internet we were relatively isolated in Irish genealogy. The only people commissioning research were from North America, Australasia, Great Britain and, occasionally, South Africa, with whom the GO corresponded on our behalf. That was done by letter, so there was rarely any personal contact.

Family history research was a pursuit alien to most Irish people. There was but one general membership organisation (open to any enthusiast) devoted to Irish genealogy – the Irish Genealogical Research Society – and most of its members lived outside the island. The same year as I began my career a new general membership organisation began in Ulster. This was the North of Ireland Family History Society. From then on genealogy very slowly developed as a popular hobby within Ireland.

Accreditation began in Ireland in the mid-1980s. Before that there were organisations offering professional credentials to genealogists but they were based in other countries and it was a long time before I heard of any of them. It is surprising to me now to know that the first such accrediting organisations were not formed until 1964, just fifteen years before I started my 'apprenticeship'. In 1979 fifteen years seemed a very long time to me. Almost forty years later it seems very much shorter. So the era of credentials for professional genealogists is not very much longer than my own career in the profession.

STARTING FROM SCRATCH

A raw beginner in ancestral research, as I was in 1979, who nevertheless has a passion for the subject and wants to pursue a career in it, needs to start moving in genealogical circles. Family history research can be pursued as a solitary endeavour, but it is easier and infinitely more enjoyable in company with people who share the love. You learn from interaction with other people and you build connections in the same way.

Assuming that you are a raw beginner, I would suggest that the first thing you do is go to an event run by a local history or family history society. Then again, that could be daunting if, like me, crowds of strangers are intimidating: so get a friend to go with you to break the ice. Once you have made some contacts within the society it will be a lot easier to attend events on a regular basis. Joining the society would be a wise step.

The genealogist in me looks at tweets from #NGS2017GEN & thinks "Must go one year!" B[u]t the introvert looks at all the peeps and says "NEVER!"

- Kassie Nelson, Historian of the American West[79]

Through mixing with other members of a society you get to know about different organisations, as well as events and publications related to genealogy. Very likely you will join other general membership societies once your network has grown. In APPENDIX B is a select list of the more prominent organisations open to all, arranged by country or specialist subject.

Your first society should not be just a stepping stone on your career path. Such organisations depend on volunteerism and altruism. Give something back: join the committee or take part in a project. Stay with that society throughout your career and help it grow. Now more than ever, genealogy needs to retain and develop its community spirit. It is more than a collection of individuals.

Attending conferences or family history fairs is important for developing your awareness of what is happening in genealogy and, in the case of the aspiring professional, for developing connections with others in the field. Nowadays, along with attending individual lectures or conferences, the most effective way to increase your knowledge is to take a course. There are all sorts of courses for genealogy or related subjects (for instance, local, oral or social history). For a select list of the more prominent ones, see APPENDIX A. These include short courses, online and correspondence courses and on-site courses. While most are taught through English, there are also French and Spanish options.

---

[79] Kassie Nelson, 'The genealogist in me ...' [Twitter post], 3.19 p.m., 10 May 2017, http://twitter.com/KassieLNelson/status/862431974987882497, accessed 18 July 2018.

There were no genealogical handbooks, no classes in genealogy to advise and educate, and no pool of experience to dip into to find out where to look next. The knowledge I accrued was in my head, an experience repeated I am sure by countless other professional and amateur genealogists tracking the same path through the sources. After that period of apprenticeship I began to feel confident enough to pass on some of the information to others by teaching.

- Stella Colwell, Family Roots: Discovering the Past in the Public Record Office (London, 1991)

While mentioning languages, I might as well make a comment here. A professional genealogist whose primary language is *not* English should *not* be expected to be able to speak that language. It is short-sighted of anglophone clients to expect them to be. The best genealogist to research one's ancestry may have no English. I would sooner engage that person, receive their report in their primary language, and engage a translator than miss out on their knowledge, skill and experience.

However, if you are a professional genealogist *not* from the anglophone world and your potential clients *are*, it may be advisable to get the basics of the English language. This is not so that you can write reports in English, or even read this book! It is so that you can understand enquiries and write a basic reply without recourse to the services of a translator. The likes of BabelFish, Bing Translator or Google Translate, which I regularly use, are not magical. They translate individual words or phrases but the sequence of translated words can often distort the meaning. So a basic course in English may be a worthwhile investment of time and money.

WHAT ARE THE ATTRIBUTES OF A TRUE PROFESSIONAL?

As I see things, there are certain attributes required by a professional genealogist. The basic ones are a passion for ancestral research and the genealogist's instinct, along with huge amounts of practical experience. What else do you need? We will assume that you have honesty and integrity. The other things I think you need are an overview of the historical context, an overview of the geographical context, an understanding of the background and structure of the records, basic competence, accuracy, precision in the use of terminology, good research skills, good computer skills and good writing skills.

An overview of the historical context:

Yes, I mean an overview. If you have a degree in history well and good, but it is not essential. An in-depth knowledge of Ancient Rome or the Medieval period will not inform your understanding of the social history of, for instance, the nineteenth century. Of course, the discipline of historical study will help, and if you have studied the nineteenth century academically that will assist your understanding of the period.

Many family history enthusiasts say that they did not like history in school. So why, later in life, did they take to personal history? That is probably it; it is personal. Kings and queens, politicians, rebels, battles and dates can be boring when put to a child. As we get older we often find that the past is an interesting place that can be explored in many ways. Local and family history are wonderful gateways to the past. With self-directed lifelong learning you can dip into whatever areas of the past that take your fancy.

However, I did say that an overview of history was needed. All the potentially boring bits about kings and queens, politicians, rebels, battles and dates do have their function. They provide a framework – a map of the past – that will help your understanding. Sadly you cannot study personal history to any great effect without putting it in a broader socio-political context. If, for instance, your ancestor was an emigrant from Ireland in the early nineteenth century it would be good to know why he or she left. It would be important to know when The Great Famine took place in Ireland to determine whether that might have been the cause. It would be good to know what was happening at the time in Australia or South Africa or Canada, or wherever they went to live, to determine what influenced their destination. That is if you are seriously researching family history as a hobby. If you intend to research professionally it is much more important that you have that map of the past.

It is important also to have a grasp of the social history of the period and location you are working in. To be able to determine the sources most likely to be relevant to an individual or family you must have an understanding of their religious, economic and social background. Also, you need to be able to recognise these circumstances in the actual records.

As well as those who did not like history in school, there are those who were interested in it but who did not choose it as an academic pursuit. In adult life they will have added to their knowledge of the subject through reading, joining historical societies, attending lectures or watching television documentaries. But, if the university of life has not provided you with an overview of history, and your study of genealogy as a hobby has failed to widen your horizons, you need to make it a priority to gain that overview.

This does not mean that you need to study everything from the Babylonians to the twenty-first century. Your work as a professional genealogist will involve certain periods of history and certain geographical areas. Do not pretend to be an expert in seventeenth century sources if this is way out of your comfort zone. Look at the areas of the past you are likely to need to deal with and concentrate on them. Follow the example of others who enjoy history and maybe study an academic course. But choose your course wisely. You need an overview covering the areas of the past you are likely to deal with. After that, if you decide to concentrate on certain aspects of those areas of the past, continue learning to your heart's content.

An overview of the geographical context:

As with the historical context, you do not need a degree in geography to be a good genealogist. What you need is to have an awareness of administrative divisions, the proximity of various locations and the physical features that may separate communities.

In Ireland, for instance, there are various administrative divisions to be understood. The established divisions were (in descending order) Province, County, Barony, Parish and Townland, with the townland consisting of a collection of farms. In the mid-nineteenth century, to these were added Poor Law Union (otherwise Superintendent Registrar's District), Registrar's District and District Electoral Division. In addition you must grasp the difference between a civil parish, a Church of Ireland parish and a Roman Catholic parish, along with their often differing areas. Getting your head around these is one of the first things an Irish genealogist must master.

Those new to ancestral research in Ireland often think narrowly about county and parish without consulting a map to determine the location of the parish within the county. They might, for example, unsuccessfully search all over County Wicklow for the marriage record of a couple who lived in Baltinglass civil parish. Had they known that Baltinglass civil parish borders both Counties Carlow and Kildare they might have expanded their search to all three counties. Had they realised that the western area of County Wicklow that includes Baltinglass is separated from the eastern coastal area of the county by a range of mountains they might have demoted eastern Wicklow to the 'less likely' category.

The boundary between two Irish counties, or even provinces, is no more than a hedge, a ditch, a stream or a river. There are four provinces in Ireland. The townlands of Corhanagh, Co. Cavan, Fihoragh, Co. Longford, and Gulladoo, Co. Leitrim, are in three different provinces, Ulster, Leinster and Connacht, respectively. However, Corhanagh, Fihoragh and Gulladoo are adjoining townlands, separated by no more than a small river and a ditch.

Having access to good maps and knowledge of the terrain are the basic requirements in relation to the overview of geographical context, no matter where you are researching.

An understanding of the background and structure of the records:

Every hobbyist must learn how each set of records they wish to use is arranged. This is pretty basic stuff that they will pick up by trial and error, if not by reading an article or a book. Anybody who has not reached that level of understanding has no business setting themselves up as a professional researcher. Unfortunately, that does not prevent some from doing so.

We will take it as read that you have figured out the structures of the main sources you need to consult, and that you have a strategy for figuring out those of the lesser-used sources. What you need beyond that is an understanding of the background of these records. This does not mean that you need to do a thesis on everything to do with the records, but you have to know something of how they came about and their original purpose.

This is particularly relevant in the case of secondary sources (or, in terms of American genealogy, derivative sources), such as indexes, abstracts or transcripts. For example, understanding something of the evolution of the 'Ireland Births and

International Genealogical Index

The *International Genealogical Index* (IGI) is a database compiled by the LDS (the Church of Jesus Christ of Latter Day Saints or Mormon church), containing references to births / baptisms, marriages and deaths of individuals from various parts of the world. It first appeared in the 1970s and was expanded over the years. It was widely available on microfiche and it became a much used research tool. Perhaps its one major problem was that it was compiled from a mixture of transcripts of *actual* records (now referred to as 'Community Indexed') and personal research by individuals (now referred to as 'Community Contributed').

In the late 1990s the LDS began a short programme of supplementary CD-ROMs under the title of *Vital Records Index* (VRI), one of which was the *Vital Records Index – British Isles,* published in 1998. A decade later the IGI was a database on FamilySearch.org, incorporating the VRI and further additional material. The IGI is still available as a database.[1] However, its 'Community Indexed' material also is available in separate databases. In relation to Ireland these consist of three databases called 'Ireland Births and Baptisms, 1620-1881', 'Ireland Marriages, 1619-1898' and 'Ireland deaths, 1864-1870'.[2]

In relation to Ireland the IGI was by no means comprehensive. However, its main advantages were that it gave details from a large proportion of civil records of birth from the introduction of registration (1864) to the late 1870s, civil records of marriage from the introduction of registration (1845) to 1870 and civil records of death, 1864-1870, as well as references from the Church of Ireland (Anglican) parish registers published in the early twentieth century by the Dublin Parish Register Society. The VRI added details from more of the civil records, as well as baptisms and marriages from many Roman Catholic parishes in Elphin diocese and many births and marriages of the Society of Friends.

---

[1] FamilySearch, 'International Genealogical Index', www.familysearch.org/search/collection/igi, accessed 18 July 2018.

[2] FamilySearch, 'Ireland Births and Baptisms, 1620-1881', www.familysearch.org/search/collection/1584963; FamilySearch, 'Ireland Marriages, 1619-1898', www.familysearch.org/search/collection/1584964; FamilySearch, 'Ireland Deaths, 1864-1870', www.familysearch.org/search/collection/1584965, all accessed 18 July 2018.

Baptisms, 1620-1881' database on FamilySearch.org would make you a better user of the source than someone who just found a 'record' on it and understood nothing of where the reference came from. Much of the database's contents came from the *International Genealogical Index*, compiled from a mixture of *actual sources* and personal research by individuals. The personal research has been filtered out, new references from the *Vital Records Index, British Isles*, have been incorporated, and additional references from civil records of birth have been included. Knowing what the main *actual sources* are and to what extent their coverage in the database is complete will prevent you from making errors when doing research for clients.

It is particularly important now that so much material is online that you understand the *actual sources*. In too many cases online databases present you with an image from a document that stands alone, out of context. Often you cannot view the previous or next page. You are given no overview. Indeed, in some cases the database is given a general name that is misleading.

Basic competence:

Familiarity with the relevant record collections and experience in using them should lead to becoming a competent researcher. The problem is that this is not always the case. Sometimes enthusiastic hobbyists-turned-'professional' just do not understand their shortcomings and have never tested their skills against any form of standards.

A client who has employed either an incompetent genealogist or a commercial firm, and who afterwards learns of gross inaccuracies in the data paid for, naturally forms a low opinion of the genealogical profession as a whole.

- Donald Lines Jacobus, Genealogy as Pastime and Profession
(New Haven, Connecticut 1930)

Unless you have learned to practice discipline over the years your research may be unsystematic. Maintaining your focus on the objective of the search is absolutely necessary. Finding lots of interesting information for a client may seem wonderful, but if that information is not relevant to their objective they are not going to share your joy.

Note taking and time keeping are very important. Beginners in genealogy find it difficult to curb their enthusiasm, so they often dive into a parish register and spend hours searching without quite knowing the dates they covered. Consequently, they find themselves repeating the same searches at a later time. Doing this kind of thing while engaged in professional research is not acceptable. If you have not managed to harness your enthusiasm you need to do something about it before considering a career in genealogy.

Accuracy:

If your report is riddled with typographical errors and wrong dates, its accuracy is completely undermined. If you cannot discipline yourself to take accurate notes and then quote them precisely in your report there is no point in thinking of a career in genealogy. This sort of error needs to be stamped out before ever taking on research for anyone else. On top of that you need to proofread any correspondence or report you issue so as to safeguard against any such errors getting through. It is always a good idea to leave aside a report for at least a day before proofreading, as you are less likely to read what you think you should see rather than the words that are actually before your eyes. One other thing: running a spell-check does not constitute proofreading.

Use of correct terminology:

If you are lax about the exact names of record repositories and collections of records the impression you give is that you will be lax about other terms or names you may use, including the client's ancestors' names and addresses. There is no need to go over the top in giving the precise name of a record collection or the title of a book every time you refer to it, and abbreviations are quite acceptable when sources are being referred to repeatedly. It is more important to be consistent in your use of terminology. There are at least three incorrect names in common use for Ireland's General Register Office. In a similar vein, with ever-increasing frequency the revision (or 'cancelled') books held by the Valuation Office in Dublin are being referred to erroneously as 'cancellation books'.

This may seem pedantic to people who regularly offend. However, this type of imprecise use of names does not inspire absolute confidence in a researcher. A report stating that such-and-such a record was examined in 'the Dublin Library' would scare off any discerning client. That is because there is no such place, and the writer of the report might mean the National Library of Ireland (in Dublin) or Dublin City Library and Archive, or indeed South Dublin County Library. If a professional genealogist is that vague about where they did the research the rest of what they write could be equally vague. If you get into the habit of using the correct terminology in everyday speech you are less likely to offend in writing.

Good research skills:

I have emphasised practical experience already. One of the things it generates is the knowledge of how to use various sources in the most effective way. Hours of slogging over records such as microfilm copies of parish registers is not entertaining. But it gives you a familiarity with these sources that cannot be substituted for by any amount of lectures. Today we have databases to do the slogging for us in most cases, so there is little opportunity to get that familiar with the records themselves. Getting to know the records intimately will make you a better researcher and will activate your genealogist's instinct to hone your personal skills.

The research skills that are generated by your genealogist's instinct and your familiarity with the records should aid your analysis of the results. You need to be able to tell the difference between possibility, probability and proven fact. If your head is muddled on this point you have a serious problem. You must be clear about these distinctions before you can move ahead to a career as a fully functioning genealogist. Perhaps you should refer to the American Genealogical Proof Standard (see SECTION 2), unless it is just going to confuse you even further.

To be able to link two pieces of information together that join two generations of a family to one another, you must have a clear understanding of the facts. If the facts leave an element of doubt you must represent this truthfully to the client. Or you must seek a way of proving the link beyond doubt. There are whole books written on this subject but part of having good research skills is the ability to determine possibility, probability and proven fact for yourself. Knowing the next steps to take in order to progress the search is another skill that instinct and experience will teach you.

Good computer skills:

It is not that long since none of us in genealogy used computers. Today they are essential. As long as you have basic knowledge of word processing for report compilation you have skills to build on. Having a much more in-depth knowledge of the finer points will enhance your report compilation. The use of footnotes and the insertion of images will make your writing more readable and add to your client's understanding and enjoyment. Of course, you also need good computer skills for online research. If you feel you are a little lost when it comes to making maximum use of your computer, a good course on the subject should be part of your preparation for becoming a professional genealogist.

Good writing skills:

Wonderfully skilful research can be rendered useless to the client by sloppy or incoherent reporting. Bad grammar, misspellings, poor punctuation, misplaced or superfluous apostrophes and an inability to construct sentences all contribute to an impression of general lack of education. Running a spell-check will do little to rectify the situation. It is worse again when the narrative is muddled and rambling. Without the ability to report coherently the genealogist is not a professional in every sense.

The task of writing a report should not be underestimated. It takes a lot of time to write one properly. Any genealogist I know will agree that report writing is equally as time consuming as the research – that is, if you report comprehensively on the search. This should be factored into your calculations when deciding on your fee. If you dash off a hasty report, with no explanation of the steps taken, the thought process, the nature of the sources consulted, the reasons why other sources were irrelevant or non-existent, the positive and negative results encountered, and the conclusions to be drawn, then the client will miss out on the benefit of the expertise for which they are paying you. Throwing in lots of citations and a draft pedigree will not substitute for explanation of how specific conclusions were reached. Your report should not merely be a response to the client personally. It should stand alone as a study of a specific problem. Not only should the client be presented with all the facts, anyone else reading it (including another professional taking up the chase) should be able to understand the extent of the search and how the conclusions were reached.

As already said, good grammar, the ability to spell, and the ability to construct sentences are vitally important in report writing. If your writing skills are not up to par you would be well advised to do a writing course before ever taking on a commission. Often a bad writer finds it difficult to give a report structure, resulting in the end-product being disjointed or going off on tangents. Again, a course is probably the most effective way to correct that problem. There are plenty of writing courses available. As well as good basic writing skills, the ability to explain the finer points of the research is essential. Once again, you need to be able to communicate to your client the distinction between possibility, probability and proven fact in particular instances.

The important thing to remember is not to despair about poor writing skills. They can be corrected. I have seen this in practice. If writing is a problem for you, work on this aspect early in your development towards a career.

TAKING THE BIG STEP

One word cannot be over-emphasised in relation to developing a career in genealogy – EXPERIENCE! There is no shortcut to acquiring it. No amount of lectures, courses, certificates, diplomas or degrees will circumvent it or compensate for it. It takes time and determination. Without having lots of experience as a hobbyist there is no good reason to begin pursuing a career in research.

However, at a certain point the dedicated hobbyist realises that they may have enough experience and expertise to be able to carry out competent research for others. If and when they decide to start taking on commissions there is no one standing over them saying that they cannot start without professional credentials (or an academic qualification); nor should there be. Making the transition from being a competent hobbyist to being a novice professional is a matter of self-belief and bravery. At that stage you have enough to worry about, dealing with clients for the first time, without needing someone else's approval. As well as that, **you have to get a track record before you can apply for professional credentials.** That track record should include the practical experience of researching on someone else's behalf, on an unfamiliar family, in unfamiliar records, and possibly dealing with a geographical area you have not researched before. In other words, you are moving outside your comfort zone and expanding your horizons. Of course, your client cannot be a guinea pig in this expansion. You need to know that you have the ability to take on these new areas and you have to allow extra research time to compensate for your slowness with unfamiliar records.

BEING WORTHY OF PROFESSIONAL CREDENTIALS

Some people may feel that because their formal education was relatively limited they are somehow unsuited to professional research, or that they need academic qualifications in order to belong to the world of professional genealogy. If this is the way you are thinking, you need to get it right out of your head. As well as being ideally suited to the Internet age, genealogy fits in nicely with the wonderful concept of lifelong learning. This encourages people of all ages to develop their knowledge in whatever way suits them, whether through attending adult education courses, studying for an academic degree, diploma or certificate, pursuing professional development in the work place or embarking on self-directed learning. Every person who takes up family history in earnest as a hobby is embarking on a self-directed journey to personal growth. So if they feel passionate enough about the subject and find that they have the genealogist's instinct they are amply suited to professional research.

If you are a born genealogist, you will sometime, somehow, find a way to devote all your time to genealogy ...

- Donald Lines Jacobus, Genealogy as Pastime and Profession
(New Haven, Connecticut 1930)

Long-term hobbyists come from a variety of walks of life and often they bring skills from a former career to bear on their practice of genealogy. Along the way they educate themselves in the subject by interacting with others (joining societies, attending conferences, volunteering for projects), by reading guide-books, magazines, journals and blogs, or indeed by attending courses. While developing in such ways they also gain practical experience of the records, especially while stepping beyond the limitations of online research. The importance of practical experience cannot be over-emphasised.

Nowadays, people in the early stages of developing a career in genealogical research sometimes think that it is a function of the accrediting bodies to supply them with a job. This is not, and never was, the case. Likewise, support

/ networking organisations are not employment agencies. There is no easy way of getting started in professional research. The route I was lucky to have open to me was an unusual one. Recruitment by institutions and research companies is relatively rare, and such entities are likely to expect applicants to have experience and (if they are blinkered) possibly academic qualifications. Most people who go into genealogical research professionally do so as self-employed sole traders. More often than not they start by doing it part-time while retaining the day job, which is understandable and advisable.

People who have run their own business, worked in accounts or run an office in their previous career are at a great advantage when beginning a career in genealogical research. This is because they have a better idea than most about setting up a business and dealing with all the non-genealogical matters that are part and parcel of a research practice. In Ireland, and undoubtedly in other countries, there are courses you can attend on setting up your own business. In the genealogy world, there is no one sitting at a desk waiting for you to come and ask questions about how to run a research business. Most of us would consider that as excessive spoon feeding. However, once you get set up there is support in some situations. The Association of Professional Genealogists (APG), the US-based support / networking (but non-accrediting) organisation, runs an annual Professional Management Conference which primarily deals with more advanced and complex issues that may be encountered, as well as research matters.

Education is a fantastic tool but, of course, the most important thing, and particularly in business, is life experience. And you can't pass exams really about business. You learn most of it from actually doing it.

- Alan Sugar, The Apprentice: You're Fired
(BBC, Series 10, Episode 7, 2015)

By the time an individual has reached the point of setting up a research business (or gaining employment as a researcher) they should have a track record of a number of years of experience in genealogy. They should have ironed out any deficiencies, such as poor writing skills. They should have figured out how to run a business and how to make research notes. Also, they should have practised report writing and honed their writing skills in this area. If they have not achieved all these essentials they are not ready to proceed.

Next they need to decide whether to run a business under their own name or (unnecessarily) pick a business name. It is important to remember that if you are promoting a business name you need also to promote your own name. After all, you want to get known as an individual in genealogy: there is no advantage in hiding behind a business name.

With a postal address, and maybe a landline telephone, you can start your business, but nowadays the other necessary tools are email and some kind of online presence. If you decide to start a blog you need to have interesting things to say every now and again. A basic website would do. If you have the money or the technical skill to create something more elaborate, well and good.

When advertising yourself, or your business, it is important to establish credibility. Remember that the potential client is taking a leap of faith in parting with their money to you, a complete stranger. Therefore, you must encourage them to choose you above anyone else who may be seeking clients alongside you. Traditionally researchers have advertised in genealogical magazines. Many still do today, but now they have an online presence as well. Magazine advertisements have little space for a sales pitch, but they should include enough to make you, the complete stranger, known to the potential client. You should include your own name and a postal address at least. A landline phone number would be additionally assuring. An advertisement giving only a business name, an e-mail address and a mobile (cell) phone number is one I would pass by without a moment's thought. There is no permanency about such details, and absolutely no guarantee to the client that this researcher will be contactable again.

Websites can be very attractively designed. Nice images and sophisticated software can project an air of professionalism and permanence. They suggest to the client that these professionals can be trusted to do a good job and to treat them fairly. But if I were looking to engage a genealogist I would not allow myself to be seduced too much by the *look* of integrity. I would search for the 'About Us' button. If it is not there I would become sceptical. Then I would search for the 'Contact Us' button. If it allows me only to complete a contact form I would become very sceptical. There may be nothing at all wrong with the anonymous stranger behind this state-of-the-art website but if they are unwilling to give information about themselves they would do without my business.

If the 'Contact Us' button has more than a contact form, again I would be looking for a personal name and a postal address, and possibly a landline phone number. An online search for information on this person may reassure me of their background beyond this website. Assuming that there is an 'About Us' button, if it just says 'we' and does not identify an actual person I am immediately turned off. If it does name a person and it gives some background information this will allow for making a better assessment of their suitability.

Whether your website is impressive to look at, it must also display integrity. As already mentioned, there should be an 'About Us' button leading to a page on which your actual name is revealed (not just 'I' or 'we'). Obviously you will want to impress with the range and extent of your knowledge and experience, but try to avoid unprofessional content.

Here are some things to avoid:

- Calling yourself an 'expert': that is an expression someone else should apply to you; self-praise is tacky and foolish.

- Stating that you are included on a record repository's list of researchers: this is not an achievement and it implies some form of recognition where there is none.

- Using post-nominal initials denoting membership of an amateur / general genealogical society anyone can join: it is bizarre for such a society to allow this and, again, it implies some form of recognition where there is none.

There is a fine line between demonstrating a wide interest in genealogy (and related fields) by listing the societies of which you are a member and suggesting to the public that membership confirms expertise. Most amateur / general genealogical societies quite rightly frown on professionals using membership as bait for clients. It is an abuse of that membership and, more importantly, it is unethical because it is misleading to the public. A step beyond unethical would be to use the emblem of such a society on your website.

By all means state that you are a member of whatever relevant organisations you belong to, and indicate any office you hold (or held) with them. This indeed demonstrates your wide interest in the subject. Just do not give the impression that membership recognises knowledge. Fellowship of such societies is an honour, which usually comes with post-nominal initials you are entitled to use. But wear them lightly, not as bait.

If you are *au fait* with social media that is a plus. It will help you build up a public profile and a network in the world of genealogy. You will find professional genealogists communicating and engaging on Facebook, LinkedIn, Twitter and beyond.

WORKING TOWARDS ACCREDITATION

Hopefully, receiving professional credentials from one of the established and internationally recognised accrediting organisations will be one of your goals. As already mentioned, you have to get a track record before you can apply for credentials. Even if you do not feel you yet have enough experience, you may be eligible to become a probationer / associate / affiliate, depending on the relevant accrediting body. This can help in working towards credentials.

Another interim option is to join a support / networking organisation. Many of them have standards of ethics by which their members must abide. The basic function of these organisations is to help their members 'network' but they also promote their members' services to the general public. They market these services through printed or online membership lists. More elaborate support organisations provide their members with more facilities. They hold meetings, publish articles and generally inform their members in business practices.

By far the largest support organisation is the Association of Professional Genealogists (APG). This US-based organisation primarily draws its membership from North America. It has become widely known outside the USA in recent years, while its membership criteria are little understood by the general public. Despite APG's guidelines to members, the appearance of the registered APG Member Logo on a website suggests to the unwary some form of credential. The logo comes with no explanation and the very name of this networking organisation is suggestive of authority. Potential clients would be forgiven for assuming that ability and experience would be criteria for membership of APG. Payment of an annual subscription (currently US$100) and an agreement to abide by the Code of Ethics are all that is required.[80] Membership of APG is, therefore, no more relevant to a genealogist's ability than membership of a local family history group. Unfortunately, more and more practitioners are choosing to join APG as a substitute for, rather than a supplement to, credentials.

[80] APG, 'Membership Dues', www.apgen.org/membership/dues.html, accessed 18 July 2018.

APG's website has the facility for clients to search for a professional genealogist by name, by location, by research specialty and by geographical specialty. The APG Code of Ethics demands honesty in dealing with clients. In addition, APG has strict guidelines on the use by its members of professional credentials, academic degrees, honorifics, honorary awards, professional learning certificates and program(me) certificates. This is to prevent the inappropriate use of post-nominal initials implying special qualifications, which may be misleading to potential clients. The guidelines specify that the letters APG should not be used as post-nominals.[81] This is why, instead of initials, you will see the APG Member symbol used by its members on stationery or websites. However, it would appear that not all of APG's members read its rules, as the initials 'APG' are to be found occasionally in use as post-nominals on social media.

Of the other support organisations for professionals, perhaps the most significant is *Verband deutschsprachiger Berufsgenealogen* [the Association of German-Speaking Professional Genealogists] (http://www.berufsgenealogie.net/) and it has restrictive membership criteria. The various French chambers / associations (see APPENDIX C i) have a different character but they might be looked on as being support bodies. There are other types of organisations from which professionals may gain support but which are not specifically for professionals.

Additionally, new practitioners may find it beneficial to join a study group which may further widen their contacts or increase their knowledge. The study groups are based in the USA and follow American practices, but they communicate online. The following is a select list of support / networking bodies and study groups, not all of which are specifically for professionals or for the field of genealogy.

- Association of Personal Historians (APH)
  www.personalhistorians.org
- Association of Professional Genealogists (APG)
  www.apgen.org
- British Association for Local History (BALH)
  www.balh.org.uk

---

[81] APG, 'Credential Guidelines', www.apgen.org/organization/policies/postnominals.html, accessed 18 July 2018.

- Federation of Probate and Asset Researchers (FPAR)
  www.fpar.org.uk
- Gen Proof Study Groups
  www.genproof.org
- Genealogical Speakers Guild (GSG)
  www.genealogicalspeakersguild.org
- International Oral History Association (IOHA)
  http://iohanet.org
- International Society of Family History Writers and Editors (ISFHWE)
  www.isfhwe.org
- International Society of Genetic Genealogy (ISOGG)
  https://isogg.org
- Professional Jewish Genealogists Group
  Contact through the conference of the International Association
  of Jewish Genealogical Societies
- ProGen Study Groups
  www.progenstudy.org
- *Verband deutschsprachiger Berufsgenealogen*
  (Association of German-Speaking Professional Genealogists)
  www.berufsgenealogie.net

If professional credentials are available in your geographical or linguistic region it would be a good idea to look at the relevant website(s) regularly for news of any changes the accrediting organisation(s) may make to the application process. Regardless of whether you qualify to apply for credentials immediately or after some time, it is good to know what is happening with the accrediting bodies. For instance, there may be an open day planned for applicants. If not, you might also try approaching an accredited professional in your area to get advice. That approach could develop into an informal mentoring process.

SURVIVING WITHOUT CREDENTIALS

At this point I should make it very clear that there are many excellent, knowledgeable and reputable professional genealogists who *do not* hold professional credentials. The accreditation processes should hold no fear for them but they have not considered it necessary to seek credentials from any organisation. This is not to say that accreditation would make these people better genealogists. It may not, but it would help potential clients in making their choice. It would also help the profession if all good professional genealogists embraced the accreditation that is available.

Surprisingly, and alarmingly, the vast majority of people calling themselves professional genealogists around the world today do not have professional credentials. For that reason there is nothing by which to measure their competence. Some, no doubt, have long experience and depend on word-of-mouth recommendations. Others may have a certificate or diploma that indicates their learning. They may feel this is equivalent to a professional credential. Some may be in the early stages of their career, and working towards applying for accreditation. In many geographical areas there is no relevant credential available. Another factor is that some of the accreditation processes are made to appear too stringent and they may scare off potential applicants. But then there are the genuinely incompetent who sell themselves as professional genealogists and who have no notion of subjecting their work to scrutiny. Their very existence within the profession is a powerful reason for promoting credentials.

APPLYING FOR CREDENTIALS

While I already stated that some of the accrediting organisations make the application process seem really daunting, applying for professional credentials is not a monstrous task. I very much like the encouraging statement from the Genealogical Institute of the Maritimes that the 'certification process is not intimidating' and that experienced genealogists 'generally have little trouble with either the work sample or the written examination'. This is the approach all accrediting bodies should take.

If you are relatively new to carrying out research for clients, applying for professional credentials should really be one of your long-term goals. You may not have all the skills needed just yet, but they can be acquired with time. If you have a passion for ancestral research and the genealogist's instinct you have the most essential attributes.

The genealogist's instinct may be innate and it usually drives a passion for the subject. On the other hand, people often have a passion for ancestral research without quite realising their shortcomings in terms of instinct and technique. A lack of instinct can be tackled with experience. This is one reason why American genealogists invest so much energy in mastering the Genealogical Proof Standard.

In the Introduction I said that there are five important hallmarks of a true professional:

- Ethics
- Knowledge
- Skill
- Experience
- Professional Credentials

Regarding **Ethics**, honesty and integrity are attributes that are instilled in most people during their formative years. Signing up to a code of ethics should be merely a declaration of having these values and taking rules of fair practice seriously. **Knowledge** needs to be acquired, but there are many ways of achieving this. **Skills** develop over time and **Experience** hones these skills, while adding new layers to knowledge. Finally, **Professional Credentials** are the stamp of approval for an all-round genealogist. *They are worth acquiring.*

Details of the various accrediting bodies for professional genealogists and their criteria are given in APPENDIX C. These organisations are:

- Accredited Genealogists Ireland (AGI)
- Association of Genealogists and Researchers in Archives (AGRA)
- Association of Scottish Genealogists and Researchers in Archives (ASGRA)
- Australasian Association of Genealogists and Record Agents (AAGRA)
- Board for Certification of Genealogists (BCG)
- *Bureau québécois d'attestation de compétence en généalogie* (BQACG)
- Genealogical Institute of the Maritimes (GIM)
- International Commission for the Accreditation of Professional Genealogists (ICAPGen)

Details of other organisations related to accreditation are given in ancillary sections of APPENDIX C, as follows:

- APPENDIX C i   Licensing in France
- APPENDIX C ii   Towards Accreditation for German-Speaking Genealogists
- APPENDIX C iii Accrediting Bodies in Specialist Areas

SECTION 4

Is Accreditation Fighting a Losing Battle?

It should be reiterated that there are many excellent genealogists who do not hold professional credentials. Yes, this has been said, but it needs to be repeated for the avoidance of doubt. I have known several such genealogists for years and I number them among my friends in ancestral research. Not all non-accredited genealogists are in that position by choice. Some do not have the option of relevant accreditation for geographical or linguistic reasons. This book is not an assault on those who choose not to (or cannot) seek credentials; it is a defence of the overall need for accreditation for the good of the general public and the profession. While there are many excellent professional genealogists who do not hold professional credentials, there are many others who are inexperienced or inept. How is the public to know the difference?

FREE-FOR-ALL?

Before the first accrediting bodies were established in 1964 professional genealogy was a free-for-all. It has to be said that at no time since then have professional credentials been universal or even in the majority worldwide, but they have been sufficiently to the fore to safeguard the general public and the profession. Before my own accrediting body in Ireland was established in 1986 Irish professional genealogy was a relatively small world, but it also was a free-for-all. There were a few people who offered their services without any idea of their shortcomings. There was nothing to distinguish fully functioning professionals from such individuals. The availability of relevant professional credentials brought stability, *not* regulation: it provided the opportunity for Irish professional genealogists to offer clients a guarantee of their competence and integrity.

In the Introduction it was stated that I believed that genealogy currently is in a state of flux. In relation to professional genealogy we have returned to the free-for-all days. The Internet has brought an unprecedented opportunity for self-marketing. A professional-looking website goes a long way when the general public are unaware of the existence of credentials in genealogy, or what they relate to. Membership of a support / networking organisation with a professional-sounding name seems as good as credentials because people hardly ever read the small print. When you can tell potential clients on your website that you have completed this 'institute' or that course it matters little to the reader how detailed or how informative it was; it gives you a 'qualification' in the eyes of the uninitiated. So why would you put yourself to the bother of jumping through all those hoops just to get credentials the general public know nothing about?

The various accrediting bodies all are administered by voluntary boards or councils or committees that put a lot of effort into running their organisations. Just doing the day-to-day chores to keep the wheels in motion is time consuming, so it is not always easy to step back and review the overall situation. I have no doubt that the following observations will be unwelcome, but they are made with a view to strengthening professional credentials. I think that the accrediting bodies may not be doing enough to tell the general public about the integrity, knowledge and experience of those they accredit. They may not be doing enough to encourage competent genealogists to seek credentials. In some cases they may even, unintentionally, be discouraging applicants by making the application process seem unachievable.

At the same time educational initiatives may, unintentionally, be undermining the whole accreditation structure. That is very likely to be an unwelcome observation too, but it seems to have foundation. Today there is a wide range of 'institutes', short courses and certificate / diploma courses, all of which should help genealogists on their way towards becoming fully equipped. However, many of those completing them feel sufficiently 'qualified' in genealogy and stop short of seeking professional credentials. When these qualifications are marketed in direct opposition to professional credentials, as with the 'Register of Qualified Genealogists', the undermining effects are obvious.

Then there is the Association of Professional Genealogists, the world's largest support / networking organisation, based in the USA. For a few decades APG had a symbiotic relationship with the two US accrediting systems. The accrediting organisations provided the professional credentials 'Accredited Genealogist' and 'Certified Genealogist' (or other grades), but they were not focused on ongoing support for those accredited. APG provided a membership framework, networking opportunities, support and CPD for people working in genealogy or related fields. These included AGs and CGs, along with those working towards professional credentials, those in related fields who were not genealogists per se (e.g., writers, publishers, archivists, librarians), and those genealogists choosing to remain outside the accreditation system.

APG is not, and does not purport to be, an accrediting organisation. It has strict guidelines for its members regarding post-nominal initials. It rightly states that 'genealogical credentials are not widely known or understood in the public sector' and that 'the public can be easily misled by inappropriate use [of post-nominals] which implies special qualifications'.[82] As mentioned previously, the guidelines outline what is acceptable use, or not, under the following headings: Professional Credentials; Academic Degrees; Honorifics; Professional Learning Certificates (awarded following rigorous courses); Program Certificates (from 'institutes' and other short courses); and Other. Included under the last heading is 'The letters "APG" are not to be positioned as a postnominal'.

This is all good. But I am suggesting that APG may, unintentionally, be damaging accreditation. Why? The problem is that, despite APG's policy and guidelines, its very name is misleading to the general public. Credentials, indeed, are not widely understood by the public. Membership of APG involves paying an annual subscription and agreeing to abide by its Code of Ethics. Members are prohibited from using 'APG' as post-nominal initials, but they may use the APG Member Logo on stationery and web pages. To the general public this logo, coupled with the organisation's name, strongly suggests accreditation.

In 2013 Catherine Desmarais wrote an article on Irish genealogy for the *Association of Professional Genealogists Quarterly* newsletter and I was one of the people she interviewed. At the time my accrediting organisation (now AGI) was called APGI and the similarity with APG was causing confusion. I was correctly quoted

---

[82] APG, 'Credential Guidelines'.

as saying 'At present [APG] is widely seen among accredited genealogists in my part of the world as providing pseudo-accreditation for beginners'. Desmarais went on to state that I 'would like to see APG express their role to consumers on the website more transparently, clearly stating the functions it does not have, such as credentialing'.[83]

At that time the statement on APG's website home page appeared to be aimed specifically at members of the public looking to engage a genealogist, and it seemed to suggest that membership of APG answered all their requirements. Now the home page is aimed primarily at 'those engaged in the business of genealogy', encouraging them to join, while it also has a perfectly reasonable section headed 'Hire an APG Professional'.[84] I am not delusional enough to think that my little remark had any bearing whatsoever on the organisation's policy, but I welcome the shift of emphasis. Unfortunately, APG's membership criteria continue to leave the organisation wide open to people of questionable ability whose APG Member Logo may be mistaken by clients as guaranteeing competence. This is how APG may, unintentionally, be damaging accreditation. Would there be so many people marketing themselves as genealogists if APG had a higher threshold for membership? The ease with which a novice may gain access to a market by joining APG must have a bearing on the rising number of the non-accredited professionals.

COUNTING PROFESSIONALS

As I mentioned already, APG had a symbiotic relationship with the two US accrediting systems. While APG has grown hugely over the years, BCG and ICAPGen have not kept pace. I was a member of APG for one year back in the early 1990s. I was at the NGS Conference in Jacksonville, Florida, in 1992 and encountered the APG stand. The organisation's functions were explained to me and I joined. Back in those dark ages, before the Internet and email brought us all closer together, I saw no real benefit in belonging to an organisation so far away, so I never renewed my subscription. However, I still have my APG *Directory of Professional Genealogists 1993*, in which I am listed with a bare postal address because I supplied no other information.

Interrogation of the *Directory* provides some interesting statistics, especially

---

[83] Catherine Desmarais, 'Genealogy in Ireland', *APGQ*, June 2013, 83.
[84] APG, home page, www.apgen.org, accessed 18 July 2018.

when they are compared with the contents of the Directory now on APG's website. Between late 2015 and early 2017 APG revised the estimate of its membership from 'more than 2,700' to 'nearly 2,800'.[85] In fact, this is something of an exaggeration, as on 5 January 2017 its membership list contained the names of 2,019 people, while on 11 April 2017 there were 2,171 names. A certain amount of fluctuation is to be expected with subscription renewals occurring throughout the year. Back in 1993 APG had a total membership of 672, so the organisation has more than trebled in size in just under twenty-five years. Its membership within the USA more or less trebled over the same period, from 587 in 1993 to 1,639 / 1,769 in (January / April) 2017. Its membership in the rest of the world grew from 85 to 380 / 402.[86]

Comparing the growth of accrediting organisations over the period 1993 to 2017 would require access to other statistics, but it is possible to compare the number of APG members in the USA who held AG and CG (or other grades) credentials in those two years. In 1993 there were 148 out of 587 American members holding professional credentials; in April 2017 only 169 out of 1,769 American members held these credentials. This suggests that accreditation in the USA almost stagnated over the quarter century, while membership of APG multiplied three-fold. It is clear that there has been a huge change in the structure of professional genealogy over the years. At some point the symbiotic interaction between APG and the accrediting systems ceased.

The vast majority of people calling themselves professional genealogists around the world today do not have professional credentials. This is not a guess: it is a fact. Leaving France, with its idiosyncratic system, out of the equation, there are eight accrediting organisations, AAGRA, AGI, AGRA, ASGRA, BCG, BQACG, GIM and ICAPGen. Again, CAFG is omitted because it relates to a niche area of genealogy. An examination of the websites of the eight accrediting bodies in early 2017 revealed that between them they then provided credentials for 723 genealogists or genealogical researchers.[87] As APG had 2,019 / 2,171 members at the same time, accredited genealogists account for no more than one third of all the professional genealogists in the world.

---

[85] APG, 'APG Welcomes APG eNews Editor' press release, 22 Dec. 2015, www.apgen.org/publications/press/2015editor.htm, accessed 18 July 2018; APG, 'About Us', www.apgen.org/about/index.html, accessed 17 February 2017.

[86] APG, 'Directory Search by Location', www.apgen.org/directory/search.html?type=location&new_search=true, accessed 5 Jan. 2017 & 11 April 2017.

[87] This number includes 50 AGRA Associates but not unaccredited AGI Affiliates or ASGRA Probationers.

Of course, not all non-accredited genealogists are members of APG. Some very good and successful professionals choose neither to seek professional credentials nor to join APG. Likewise, it must be said that very many accredited genealogists are not members of APG, so those with professional credentials may make up an even smaller proportion of the overall world population of professional genealogists. In April 2017, APG had 25 members between the Republic of Ireland and Northern Ireland. These included only three Members and two Affiliates of Accredited Genealogists Ireland. AGI's membership then stood at 37, along with eight (non-accredited) Affiliates. Similarly, the two Canadian-based accrediting bodies listed a total of 112 people holding their credentials and BCG listed five Canadians holding its credentials. By comparison APG had 71 Canadian members.

Also in April 2017, some 217 US genealogists held professional credentials from BCG and 148 held them from ICAPGen. Some people held both, so the individuals holding either credential numbered slightly less than 365. At the same time only 169 of those accredited individuals in the USA were members of APG. It is no longer the case that APG represents the majority of American genealogists holding professional credentials, if it ever did. Likewise, APG's non-accredited members now outnumber those with professional credentials by 1,600. This should be of concern for BCG and ICAPGen. Clearly the ideals that gave birth to the terms 'Accredited Genealogist' and 'Certified Genealogist' in 1964 have been forgotten. It appears that professional credentials nowadays are regarded as one of a number of options rather than as an essential for any self-respecting professional.

TEST OF SKILL OR OBSTACLE?

APG may, unintentionally, be weakening professional credentials in the USA, but there are other possible causes for the American accrediting bodies not attracting more applicants. One of these must be laid at the door of the accrediting bodies themselves.

It is important to have rigorous standards if a credential is to mean anything. Applicants need to understand that they must achieve a level of expertise to gain a credential and that this is not easy. The public need to know that the credential guarantees that level of expertise. However, there is rigorous and then there is insurmountable! Compared with the application criteria for the other regional accrediting organisations, those of BCG and ICAPGen are discouraging, to say the least.

Just reading through the descriptions of the BCG and ICAPGen application processes is exhausting. There is nothing about these processes that seems inviting or encouraging. Worse than that is the fact that the processes need to be repeated every five years during a career in genealogy. None of the other six regional accrediting bodies have such requirements, and perhaps BCG and ICAPGen should consider their purpose. Yes, technology changes access to records continuously and rapidly, but a genealogist's instinct, knowledge and experience do not have to be recharged every five years. Other professions do not demand such excessive measures of their practitioners and they generally employ continuing professional development (CPD) to keep their credentials relevant.

I can see how the American accreditation systems would be off-putting even to the most self-respecting professional. I bet that if the five-year renewal was replaced by a commitment to CPD it would bring a lot more genealogists into the fold. Encouraging people to seek credentials should be one of the objectives of all accrediting bodies, because this helps to protect standards and credibility for the profession as a whole.

Sometimes it is not a bad thing to be told some home truths. Several years ago my own accrediting body was talked about by some in Irish genealogy as 'elitist'. That was a shock for us, as we thought we were encouraging new applicants. Following that we introduced an informal mentoring process for potential applicants. More recently we introduced a formal Affiliate programme. Most new Members now come through that programme.

As mentioned already, I am particularly impressed by the 'Overview of the Certification Process' on the website of the Genealogical Institute of the Maritimes (GIM). It includes the following:

> *The certification process is not intimidating. Genealogists experienced in researching primary or original record sources, secondary or printed sources, and in analyzing and evaluating genealogical facts, and who have learned to cite or footnote sources, generally have little trouble with either the work sample or the written examination.*[88]

This is how accreditation should be presented to potential applicants.

The other thing that accrediting bodies probably need to work harder on is marketing the expertise of those they accredit. Perhaps some of them think this is not their responsibility, but surely it is! If the general public does not know

---

[88] GIM, 'Guide for Certification', http://nsgna.ednet.ns.ca/gim/wordpress/?page_id=668, accessed 18 July 2018.

the difference between a professional credential and membership of a support / networking organisation or having a diploma for completing a course, the credential is of limited value to its holder. The accrediting organisations need to raise their profiles and explain what their credentials mean.

OTHER OPINIONS

As someone who began his career at a time when there was no relevant professional credential for Irish genealogists, I see the need for promoting good genealogists and protecting clients in the tried and tested way. Unfortunately, today potential clients worldwide remain as confused as ever about the way to identify a good genealogist. In my opinion, professional credentials are the stamp of approval for genealogists with integrity, knowledge, skill and experience. The various accrediting bodies may be in need of some soul-searching but the credentials they grant are important to genealogy as a profession.

The credentials are enabling rather than regulating. They are available to anyone with the necessary competence but there is no compulsion to obtain them. They do not restrict recognition to those with academic qualifications. Indeed, they confirm abilities beyond academic learning in that they affirm all-round knowledge, skills and experience, regardless of the route the genealogist has taken to achieve them.

That is my opinion, but I am interested to hear and understand other views. I found one opposing take on the situation online, that of Lisa B. Lee. She describes herself as a computer professional who 'combines her extensive computer skills with her love for genealogy to help clients maximize the wealth of digital information available online'. She does not have professional credentials in genealogy but she holds a PLCGS (Professional Learning Certificate in Genealogical Studies) from the National Institute for Genealogical Studies in Ontario. She owns the website Got Genealogy?[89]

In a paper given at the inaugural MAAGI (Midwest African American Genealogy Institute) in 2013 she addressed the topic 'Certification: Is it Really Necessary?'. In the hand-out for the lecture[90] she summarised some of the professional accreditation and established courses available in North America.

---

[89] *Got Genealogy?*, 'About Got Genealogy?', http://gotgenealogy.com/about-got-genealogy/, accessed 18 July 2018.
[90] *Got Genealogy?*, 'Is Certification Necessary?', http://gotgenealogy.com/wp-content/uploads/2013/07/MAAGI-Certification.pdf, accessed 18 July 2018.

She quite rightly pointed out that professional credentials are not needed in order to take on research commissions. She suggested taking classes and advised expanding horizons by taking a course in an unfamiliar area of research.

In relation to BCG she commented that the 'fact that the BCG keeps the identity of the judges a mystery makes absolutely no sense to me, and it takes away from their credibility'. She pointed out that if applying for a PhD she would know the identity of the person assessing her work. Lee further observed: 'Some of the best genealogists on the planet ... have neither an AG or a CG ... and I'm not the only one who has marveled at how a particular genealogist acquired his/her AG or CG.'

It would be a bit rich for me to take exception to forthright opinions! To an extent I understand Lee's views, but I think we might all marvel at how certain people hold all sorts of qualifications, including academic degrees: that observation is not confined to professional credentials in genealogy. I fundamentally disagree with her on the issue of maintaining the anonymity of those adjudicating on an application for professional credentials. It is not necessary to know the identity of any individual assessor once it is established that all assessors are of a particular standing. BCG has a panel of judges, all of whom are CGs. Therefore, having achieved that status, they should be competent to assess applications. In addition, being bound by BGC's Code of Ethics and Conduct, they are required to behave honourably towards those being assessed.

My own organisation, AGI, has a panel of independent assessors. Their identity is not a secret, but the identity of the three assessors evaluating any particular application is known only to the chair-holder of the panel. There is a practical reason for this. As genealogy is quite a small world, particularly in Ireland, it is possible that the applicant may know an assessor personally. It would be unfair to the assessors to expose them to canvassing from active applicants or resentment from those unsuccessful.

To obtain a greater cross-section of opinions on the issue of professional credentials for genealogists, I asked a number of professionals to respond to a questionnaire. These were individuals of standing, divided into two groups – ten without credentials and ten with credentials. Both groups had people from various locations spread across North America, the British Isles, Continental Europe and Australasia. I began this process in 2014, when I started preparing to write this book. I wanted honest and forthright answers. For that reason, when asking people to participate, I promised that their names would not be revealed.

The two categories were as follows:

10 *Without* Professional Credentials

These individuals had been active in genealogy for periods of between 16 and 48 years, and had been practising as professionals for between 18 months and 41 years.

10 *With* Professional Credentials

These individuals had been active in genealogy for between 11 and 44 years and had been practising as professionals for between four and 35 years. Their professional credentials were from seven of the accrediting bodies. Two individuals had credentials from two bodies.

Initially it was my intention to write a summary of the themes that arose. Having read the detailed answers I felt that the respondents' own words were worth reproducing. The summaries below are edited slightly, merely for greater clarity.

WITHOUT PROFESSIONAL CREDENTIALS

Q. Have you ever contemplated applying for professional credentials?

RESPONSE: Yes 8; No 1; Ambivalent 1

Q. Have you ever applied for professional credentials?

RESPONSE: Yes 4 (including 1 in process); No 1; Ambivalent 1

Q. Have you ever had professional credentials?

RESPONSE: Yes 1; No 7; Ambivalent 2

Q. Did any of the following contribute to you not holding credentials from one of the international accrediting organisations?

A) Geographical location

RESPONSE: Yes 2; No 7; Not Applicable 1

- [repeated below] Yes, but I don't know if it is really interesting for a Spanish-speaking researcher; all the organizations that offer credentials are for English-speaking and French-speaking professional genealogists... and there are important differences between researching in Spain or Latin-America and in England or the USA or France.

- My main reason for not having credentials is that for a long time, I did not know that credentialing organizations existed. Here in [a Continental European country], there are no credentialing organizations. It wasn't until I started working for clients in the US that I became aware of the possibility.

B) Primary language

RESPONSE: Yes 1; No 8; Not Applicable 1

- [repeated from above] Yes, but I don't know if it is really interesting for a Spanish-speaking researcher; all the organizations that offer credentials are for English-speaking and French-speaking professional genealogists... and there are important differences between researching in Spain or Latin-America and in England or the USA or France.

C) Full-time employment outside genealogy precluded you from applying

RESPONSE: Yes 2 (1 as in too busy; 1 possibly same); Possibly 1; No 6; Not applicable 1

D) Type of work within genealogy precluded you from applying

RESPONSE: Yes 0; Not exactly 1; No 8; Not applicable 1

E) Saw no need for credentials

RESPONSE: Yes 6; Somewhat 1 (as genealogy time limited); No 3

- Yes, in view of the work I was doing.

- Probably because of my own experience, I do consider qualifications of some sort are essential - especially the concept of time management on jobs.

F) Requirements seemed unattainable

RESPONSE: Yes 0; No 8; Not applicable 2

G) Aversion to the application criteria

RESPONSE: Yes 1; No 7; Ambiguous 1; Not applicable 1

- Yes, the application process was very basic and did not meet my definition, nor expectation, of professional.

- I did look at an application for BCG (many years ago), one of the criteria for Irish research was analyzing an eighteenth century deed among gentry. I didn't think this was relevant to the typical Irish research case, which usually involved non-landowning tenant farmers. I felt that BCG was a bit "behind" in their knowledge of that field (at that time, anyway).

H) Aversion to the adjudication process

RESPONSE: Yes 1; No 8; Not applicable 1

- Yes, at the time BCG had no Canadians to adjudicate Canadian applications.

- British Isles – No, I approve of it.

- I do not normally undertake paid research. I therefore decided that AGRA was not really relevant to what I was doing. There is, perhaps, scope for an organization for those of us who are professional genealogists, but do not undertake paid research. But I probably would not get involved in such an institution, if one were created, at this stage in my life.

J) Aversion to the renewal criteria [only practised by BCG and ICAPGen]

RESPONSE: Yes 2; No 8

- Canada / BCG – Again part and parcel of previous statements: process basic & adjudicators should be from the country of the applicant.

- Yes, somewhat of a concern after I stopped doing client research/ reports. Assessments would have been the only work product I could submit for renewal.

- While this did not prevent me from applying, I think the BCG requirement to submit a portfolio every 5 years is very demanding. There are a lot of great genealogists who do not take client work or publish articles, for whom compiling a portfolio is a lot of extra work. BCG have updated their standards manual for the first time in 14 years, so if people have shown that they meet these standards they shouldn't be required to renew so quickly.

K) Were there other reasons?

'I did not know that credentials existed before 2012.'

RESPONSE: Yes 5; No 5

- Yes, as mentioned I felt that adjudicators should be from the country of the applicant, and at the time of my application there were Canadian members, but none were allowed to adjudicate.

- I did not know that credentials existed before 2012.

- Mainly, I really liked researching for clients, but I spent an inordinate amount of time on the reports – which I did not enjoy. I also didn't feel I could charge the same rate for the report prep as for the research, so I set a standard report fee. I finally determined that it was not worth my investment of time. So, I changed my primary focus to working with my clients, doing an assessment, followed by onsite assistance. This was much more rewarding overall.

- Working full-time as a genealogist, dependent entirely on genealogical income for food, shelter, and insurance, as well as already donating extensive volunteer time to genealogical organizations, simply left little time for the work involved in the credential process.

- The attitude of many that have credentials seems to be that no one else is capable of doing the work without giving the individual a chance to prove they can.

L) How do you think the relevant organisation(s) could make the **attaining of professional credentials** more attractive?

'More marketing to genealogists so people know that credentialing organizations exist. More marketing to clients so people know where to find a credentialed professional, which makes the credential more valuable.'

'I think it will be very interesting offering Spanish-speaking people the possibility of obtaining a credential, making the process in Spanish or addressing the peculiarities of Hispanic research.'

- For many years I have pondered this question. Personally I would like to see a standard set of questions about knowledge of locating resources, methodology and interpretation of records. When we go to a doctor we expect certain basic standards to be common knowledge among all of them, and then many of them have become specialists. The same is true of a lawyer, or a computer technician – there are basics. Many genealogists who have professional credentials still contact me personally or come into my archives and ask me questions that they should have been taught.

- This is a delicate balance. If it is too easy, it increases the number of applicants (and the revenue to the certification body), but it diminishes the value and "prestige" for lack of a better word. I don't feel it should be too attractive.

- To me it seems that those that are certified could make a better effort on how they conduct their conversations with those who are not certified. Maybe those of us that are not are waiting for a time in life when they might be able to have the time it takes to commit to the project of applying. Instead, the not certified genealogists mostly get the attitude that we are not worthy to be in the field. My feelings are not for all that are certified, I have many friends that are and they do not act that way. But, I think we have created too much of a divide at this point that it will be hard to bring the two sides together.

- More marketing to genealogists so people know that credentialing organizations exist. More marketing to clients so people know where to find a credentialed professional, which makes the credential more valuable. More educational opportunities in [Continental] Europe where genealogists can educate themselves about methods and standards (like GRIP, SLIG in US) and see how credentialed professionals work.

- In my case, I think it will be very interesting offering Spanish-speaking people the possibility of obtaining a credential, making the process in Spanish or addressing the peculiarities of Hispanic research.

M) How do you think the relevant organisation(s) could make the application process more attractive?

- I am only familiar with the application process of two, BCG and ICAPGEN, but it appears that the general perception of ICAPGEN is that it is primarily for the LDS, although that is not the case. The process does appear simpler for ICAPGEN than BCG, especially since I make two 9-day research trips to Salt Lake City each year. However, it is the time commitment that prevents me from applying for credential – not the process itself.

- Not sure – possibly through my own lack of knowledge of most of them.

- I do not know, I have not looked.

- Supporting more languages so people can submit portfolios in their native language. If that isn't possible (e.g. not enough judges yet) make sure the rubrics are such that the skills being tested are genealogical, not the ability to write perfect English. Having mentors that help new applicants. Not requiring on-site exams like ICAPGEN. Having standards manuals in multiple languages. Providing examples of high quality work in multiple languages. Breaking up the application process. For example, BCG could allow applicants to submit the portfolio in two parts. That would mean that the candidates receive feedback sooner and don't have to do all the work if they're clearly not ready, and can show improvement in their second half. Relaxing renewal requirements.

N) More detailed observations would be welcome – feel free to elaborate as much as you wish.

- Since I am now slowly trying to simplify my life, including eliminating the number of boards of directors and offices that I hold, I am not sure of any major benefits for me to obtain my CG and CGL at this time. I have been encouraged by CGs to apply.

- While I do believe that a credential in any field can be a definite plus, I have been able to maintain a full-time client base with the reputation and referrals that my past research, teaching, speaking, and writing have produced. I do not feel I have suffered any significant discrimination or loss of opportunity for lack of a credential. All my comments pertain to professional genealogy in the US, where all my experience has been. Having been very active with several of the national genealogical organizations and institutes, as well as a state society, I am well aware of how political they are at their core, like almost any organization. I do believe that both ICAPGen and BCG do a credible job of keeping the politics out of the credentialing process for individuals. However, the process of establishing and revising credentialing criteria has certainly been strongly political, as is the process of determining leadership and control of both organizations.

- I believe BCG took a long-needed step several years back in simplifying its categories so that basically a certified person is a "Certified Genealogist," much more understandable to the general public than the previous range of certified categories. But the process they used, grandfathering in CGRSs [merging the categories] who had not yet met the CG criteria, was in my opinion greatly flawed, and devalued the CG credential.

- The genealogical field overall has changed dramatically, but in many ways seems to become more fragmented all the time. That is also true of professional genealogy in the US. It was an unfortunate missed opportunity for the field of genealogy when the Family

History Library dropped the AG process and ICAPGen was formed. It was the best chance for organizations to combine the accrediting and certifying processes and establish one basic credential for professional genealogy, which could have been a strong and effective force in the field. As it is, APG, BCG, ICAPGen, and non-affiliated professionals remain separate but often overlapping in their efforts, and their voices, concerns, and effectiveness remain unnecessarily dispersed and diluted. One final observation: as with this survey, obviously another factor in my not working toward a credential is my own procrastination. There always seem to be too many other priorities and things to do.

· In [a Continental European country], most people will speak and write English but I don't think there are many genealogists who are fluent enough in English to write whole articles, let alone a whole portfolio. I discussed this with a fellow genealogist, who works at the largest genealogical library in [this country], the other day and he agreed with me that it is just too difficult for most people. Also, the standards being tested against are unknown here. Genealogical education and publications in [this country] are very source-oriented. Since we have so many excellent sources, the suggested solution for any research problem is always: find more records. There is hardly any focus on analysis or quality of sources beyond the general advice to use original records instead of indexes. I think genealogy education as a whole needs to be a lot more mature before more people will be open to or ready for obtaining credentials. It's only when people know there are standards and methods that they will want to know whether they are applying them correctly.

· I did a Diploma of Family History Studies with the Society of Australian Genealogists at the beginning of the 1980s. In those days this was the accepted qualification to work professionally. It involved a 'short' thesis which highlighted particular sources, a 'long thesis' on a family who had been in Australia for about four generations, a two-hour exam (which in those days involved the option of some heraldry), etc. I then went on to supervise candidates for many years - all my students who got to the last submission got through but I did lose some along the way who found the theses too much. In those days it was mainly working under your own impetus and some could not do that. Over the years the requirements were extended, right down to a 'phony' job for which they had to submit invoices, etc., so I think it was most useful.

· Also I think it useful to have a smattering of disciplines outside your own family experience. I think because of the Australian immigrant experience it is essential to have had some experience in researching in other countries but then again not everyone can experience this. These days a website component would be essential. Also I would not be opposed to a regulated 'updating' process over the years. The game has changed significantly since I had my first client. On the other hand I would always contend that a basic knowledge of history of the region would never be luggage to carry and could only assist. But if asked the main 'qualification' to undertake research, I would always maintain 'a knowledge of sources': where they are, how each one was developed, and what can be learned - or expected - from each one. Active work in repositories imparts this knowledge.

· Once I knew that BCG existed, I knew I wanted to apply. My main reasons are: I want to know whether I measure up to standards; the portfolio work plus feedback from the judges is an amazing educational opportunity; I think having credentials would make it easier to get US clients with more complex, long-term projects; I think having credentials would showcase my skills to fellow genealogists, which would lead to interesting contacts and possibly referrals; I think having credentials would make it easier to be invited as a speaker in the US.

· At first, I didn't know about the standards in use in the US. It took me about a year to become familiar enough with those standards to feel confident enough to submit my initial application. I plan to submit my portfolio [soon]. Compiling a portfolio is a lot of work, especially for people like me who do this besides a part-time job, running a business and raising a family. Being 'on the clock', I am a member of the BCG action mailing list for applicants. I was shocked to see how many people are on the clock compared to how many people get credentials.

There are dozens per year who join the group, but only a few people each year receive their credentials. The ratio is at least 10 to 1. I heard that about 1 in 3 pass on their first try, so this must mean that most people that submit their initial application never get to the point of submitting their portfolios. I think some realize they are not ready, and for others it is just too much work. That's why I think it would be good to have a smaller first step, so people get feedback sooner and know if they're on the right track.

WITH PROFESSIONAL CREDENTIALS

Q. What were your main motivations for seeking professional credentials?

'It greatly enhanced my impact with the professional genealogical community in the US in relation to my full-time employment.'

'... because I thought it was the right thing to do.'

- I wanted to test myself against the standards in the field and receive peer review of my work from the strongest genealogists in our field.
- It greatly enhanced my impact with the professional genealogical community in the US in relation to my full-time employment.
- My overall motivations were to increase my skill sets and to push myself to be a better genealogist.
- I saw professional credentials as an integral part of becoming a professional genealogist. Credentials would allow me to practise as an equal with other accredited professionals, thereby assuring potential clients of a high standard of service and ethics. It would also allow me to charge a realistic fee for my services.
- To enable clientele to have confidence in my expertise and ensure that my standards were at least the minimum required by a professional body.

- Both programs [AG & CG] increase your skills in different areas and complement each other.

- I wanted to see if I had the skills and ability to meet the rigorous standards of BCG.

- In France, without a professional credential you do not have a professional card, and without a professional card you do not get access to registries and therefore cannot do any type of research under 75 years.

- In France, being part of a professional chamber means to be part of a community of professional genealogists getting access to all the relevant information on new legislations and on the industry. The professional chamber subscribes to an insurance which covers the work of all its members in terms of research (equivalent to MBI: Missing Beneficiary Indemnity). To be part of a professional chamber meant recognition by our clients and more trust conferred to us with such credentials.

- Being employed as the Director of [a research centre], I believed it was incumbent upon me to achieve some visible level of competency, thus I sought membership of [the relevant accrediting body].

- To be seen to be professional and competent; because I thought it was the right thing to do.

- In order to establish my bona fides as a professional genealogist; so that colleagues would recognise me as a peer. For my own gratification too, if I'm honest; I wanted to prove to myself that I "made the grade".

2) Do you feel credentials are important for professional genealogists? If so, why?

'It has been my experience, and the expressed experience of other credentialed genealogists, that once credentialed one tends to receive larger, more complex cases requiring advanced evidence-evaluation skills.'

- Yes, to ensure that professionals are competent at what they do and that they have taken steps to test themselves against a minimum standard. Also gives an assurance to clients and helps to make the profession more credible.

- Yes. It should give those seeking help in their research some confidence in the quality of such help.

- There are some specific situations in which credentials are particularly important, or even required, such as forensic work that will be presented in court, expert witness testimony, US military repatriation research, and some applications for university scholarships where documentation of lineage is required. That aside, in more general terms and like credentials in any other field, it is an identifier for the public. It's an indicator of competence to the genealogy-consuming public. It doesn't mean that genealogists without a credential are not competent, it merely provides the public with an indicator that this particular person's work has been vetted. This sometimes results in benefits to the individual credential-holder. It has been my experience, and the expressed experience of other credentialed genealogists, that once credentialed one tends to receive larger, more complex cases requiring advanced evidence-evaluation skills.

- It depends – credentials are important in certain arenas and are mandatory in others. For example, if you are an expert witness in the US, then the credentials establish your credibility as a witness. They indicate that you have met a particular standard of practice and your peers acknowledge your competency in the subject area. Also I feel that when you have clients, the code of ethics you sign as a professional genealogist with the accrediting bodies and their commitment to mediate differences between the professional and the client provide a credible benefit to all clients even if they don't need to mediate any issues.

- I do feel they are important, both for the professional genealogist and for the potential clients, who need to know that they are hiring a genealogist with standards and recognised expertise.

- Yes. For several reasons. First, because it shows potential clients that you have met the standards of your peers. Second, because it shows you are able to perform quality research in a reasonable amount of time in the area in which you claim expertise. Third, because it shows that you ascribe to a set of standards and a code of conduct that is monitored by the credentialing organization. If you do something underhanded, the client can report you to the organization and can expect the complaint to be investigated.

- We feel it is very important in order to be credible to clients recognizing us as professional genealogists and not just scam (as there are too many); it is also important as it insures the rightful proceeding of genealogists, insuring a certain level of professionalism.

- Without doubt, I believe this. They establish recognisable standards which can safeguard the interests of clients and establish that the holder of such credentials is knowledgeable and their work can be relied upon. Genealogy seems to attract an unfortunate number of those who might provide a professional service at an amateur level. Obtaining credentials has assisted me greatly in this regard.

3) **What are the main strengths of your credentialing body / bodies in terms of eligibility, assessment process and maintenance of credentials?**

- Membership of AGI is open to all who match the qualifying criteria: those who have worked full time for at least one year (or two years part time), accepting clients on a fee-paying basis, may submit a sample of their work for consideration by the independent Board of Assessors. There is no "peer review" in AGI. All applications are dealt with by Assessors and this is much to AGI's credit. Ireland is a small place and one tends to know or know of almost all others working in the field.

- AGRA has a minimum standard and assessment process for applicants, only those who have reached the required standard are eligible for membership.

- AAGRA has a fairly stringent peer examination system. The candidate must submit some completed research projects and if the examining panel sees any anomalies, i.e. poor citations or misleading information, they will return the submitted documentation and the candidate will be asked to do better.

- ASGRA now has 4 categories of membership, allowing for flexibility as years and situations evolve. ASGRA applicants are peer-assessed, ensuring a universal standard within the association. The application process gives credit to professionalism, expertise and experience in candidates who may or may not have undertaken a post-graduate course in genealogy, while also embracing those candidates who *have* taken a course, but who may not be as experienced in terms of years. Submitted samples of work are assessed on a scoring basis, which is subjected to a standardisation process on a regular basis. Part of our assessment process is an interview, which is also useful for ascertaining personability, which is an important attribute for anyone running a practice of any kind. ASGRA operates a complaints procedure. Also, along with AGRA, ASGRA members have the opportunity to practise CPD, although this is not mandatory, through study days and membership of Regional Network Groups. There are no age limits on membership of ASGRA.

- BCG – While this is basically an open book exam, it focuses on the quality of your work product and your expertise is illustrated in the variety of sources used in your compilations and the skill with which you have solved indirect evidence problems. You are not truly a professional genealogist if you cannot solve indirect evidence genealogical problems and the approach to this by BCG adequately tests that ability. It also includes a publication format that until recently worked well for clients. My personal opinion is that it now needs to come into the twenty-first century and include interactive graphics, illustrations and the establishment of family websites if that is what the client desires.

- BCG – 1. Objectivity of the standards and rubrics used to evaluate portfolios; 2. multiple assessors: three judges plus a fourth judge when the three judges are not in agreement; 3. the judges are some of the strongest leaders in our field – published authors and well-respected speakers and researchers; 4. the array of projects in the portfolio allows for a sufficient opportunity to demonstrate a wide range of skills; 5. no one can coast once they are certified. Peer review of a credentialed person's work is ongoing.

- BCG – Judgment is done by a blind panel of three certified genealogists, with a fourth called in to settle any discrepancies. The organization is constantly reviewing the credentialing process to improve it. Judges' names are kept confidential so no one knows who is on the panel of judges, which is good for the process. There are a number of rubrics that a new applicant is measured against. It is a fair process.

- In France, the main strengths are the level of professionalism, knowledge of the industry and experience in this industry that one needs to show first of all to get the credential. Then each member will be reviewed on a regular basis to ensure their level of professionalism is maintained to the level expected by the chamber.

- ICAPGen – The credentialing process requires a timed exam, which is different from BCG. This demands that you actually know the material, that you have exercised the requisite 1,000 hours of research in the area of specialty, and quickly weeds out candidates that are not ready to research in the area. This, coupled with the document recognition portion of the exam tells the adjudicator that you have a grasp of all of the major record sources for the area of specialty. All of this is followed by an oral board of review of your peers which also tests your ability to respond orally and indicates your ability to think under pressure, organize your thoughts, develop a research plan and review the appropriate source materials.

4) What are the main weaknesses of your credentialing body / bodies in terms of eligibility, assessment process and maintenance of credentials?

'The main weakness is the lack of recognition of the credential, as much as the credential body, outside the borders of France.'

- I don't believe AAGRA's system has any real weaknesses. In reviewing their work a candidate should have the skills to find and correct their own errors.

- BCG – 1. Some subjectivity unavoidably can creep in, despite efforts to avoid it; 2. insufficient opportunity to correct areas of weakness, "all or nothing" process: one can only resubmit an entirely new portfolio, not just the weak pieces; 3. the renewal period is short; 4. no continuing education requirement.

- ICAPGen – The process requires that you be onsite at one of the specified locations. While this may seem like an inconvenience, the testing points align with where the professional should be conducting research in the major archives/libraries. The renewal process covers ground already previously tested and requires a research project even for those who are not currently working with clients. Since the renewal occurs every five years, this ability has been adequately tested a number of times.

- BCG – The same renewal issues are relevant for BCG. As opposed to ICAPGen where you meet those reviewing your testing results in the oral board of review, you have no idea who has reviewed your packet. In some specialty areas, the person being tested may be a far better expert than those reviewing the submitted materials. In my case, my transcription of the testing document was more accurate than the template being used to adjudicate the results.

- The main weakness is the lack of recognition of the credential, as much as the credential body, outside the borders of France.

- AGRA – The guidance notes and application process need some revision to remove some ambiguities in how applications should be submitted and with what samples of work.

- ASGRA does not have an external overseeing moderator. Also it does not have a structure for the maintenance of credentials. With currently 21 members, associates and probationers, it is a small association, which could be seen as a weakness, or there again as a strength, indicating the stringency of our assessment process.[91]

- AGI – Because the process has evolved one of the main weaknesses is consideration by the Assessors can take too long. We have fairly

---

[91] ASGRA has made some changes since these comments were made.

recently begun to utilise CPD. This might be better if one had to attend a minimum per year on a compulsory basis.

- AGRA – 1. Not well regarded in the field (it was badly run for many years and had an elitist reputation); 2. members make up only a small proportion of the number of professional genealogists practicing in England and Wales; 3. traditionally it has a close relationship with the IHGS whose courses are rather old fashioned.

5) Anything you would change about the credentialing criteria or processes of your credentialing body / bodies?

- AGI – Yes, I would completely overhaul the process as regards the input from the Assessors. We should significantly increase the application fee to discourage premature applications.

- BCG / ICAPGen – My personal opinion is that we do not need two credentialing bodies in the United States – that [may] draw immediate criticism from both sides, but the truth is that we have one American Medical Association. You either pass their test or you are not a practicing doctor in the US. We could do the same if the two sides would come together.

- BCG – The renewal period could be lengthened, especially if a continuing education requirement was instituted. Also, it would be worthwhile to consider allowing one or two especially weak parts of a portfolio to be redone, if it would make a difference in the portfolio passing or not, rather than needing to submit an entirely new portfolio.

- BCG – The organization seems to change the requirements quite a bit lately and it has been hard to keep up with for those who have been credentialed for a while. It almost seems like they are changing things just to change things in the assessment process. I think they need to leave things alone for a while and see how they shake out.

- AGRA – The process could be made simpler without reducing the requirements of making an application.

- AGRA – 1. They are about to 'tighten' admission procedures – the problem is that it will exclude people like me who can walk the walk, but have never talked the talk; 2. it also makes it difficult for non-genealogical history researchers to join (which makes a mockery of its title).[92]

- ASGRA – The criteria and processes are continually being adjusted, to suit changes in the genealogy world, so I have no worries there. We will never suit everyone, but that is another issue.

6) Would you suggest a better set of eligibility criteria? Elaborate as you wish.

- No. I believe the AAGRA system to be quite adequate. However I am not familiar with many others in the world.

- AGRA – Make it as open as possible.

- AGI – These days there are so many "wannabe" professional genealogists, I would be of a mind to raise the period working in the field to two years full-time before an application can be submitted.

- ASGRA has recently added a new category of membership, to allow non-practising genealogists, employed in a related area, to become affiliated to the association. This was in response to demand from the academic world. We continually look at our eligibility criteria, and are satisfied at present that they are in keeping with current trends.

- BCG / ICAPGen – Both programs need to test for a very dynamic electronic era in which the client needs are different than they were when the programs were established. As far as I can see, the credentialing bodies keep telling the client what they need rather than listening to what clients desire. Clients want a way to share their family history with their families in the way they want to consume it – today that is electronic for family members under the age of forty.

- BCG – While there may be minor things that could be improved, on the whole it is a fair and well-thought-out process.

7) Would you suggest a better adjudication process? Elaborate as you wish.

- BCG – It would be worthwhile to consider a double-blind process, where both the judges and the applicant were both unknown to the other. Now it is a single-blind process where the judges are unknown

---

[92] AGRA has made some changes since these comments were made.

to the applicant but the applicant is identified on the portfolio being judged. There are pros and cons to making it double-blind, though.

- BCG / ICAPGen – I actually like the adjudication processes of the two organizations overall, but I would like to see more transparency in the BCG process.

- AGRA – I would like to see adjudicators to be external to the organisation to ensure that there is a consistent and independent approach to assessment of applications.

- By adjudication I assume you mean assessment? ASGRA has an assessment panel of 3 full members, on a rotating chairman basis. We undertake to complete the application process within 6 weeks. The assessors are not necessarily Council members and therefore our process is not elitist. The assessors meet to standardise on their assessments and success of application is by a unanimous decision. The process is fairly traditional, no gimmicks, and I think we have it about right for our type of association.

- AAGRA – Only a secondary questionnaire re some general fields of records that were perhaps not covered in the original submitted subject matter. As a record agent I find the knowledge of what records are available and what is in those records to be of utmost importance.

8) **Do you think those with credentials should have to renew their credentials periodically? [only practised by BCG and ICAPGen] Elaborate as you wish.**

- BCG – I do. Demonstrating one's continued growth is essential to show one has kept up with changes in the field, and is continuing to work to standards. The field of professional genealogy is a young one, and a rapidly changing one. Standards are improving, and technology is expanding at a phenomenal rate. Without renewal of credentials, a person who had become credentialed decades ago could still be advertising themselves as credentialed despite not knowing how to access digitized records, or being knowledgeable about newly available records, or understanding current standards of source documentation or genealogical proof. Other professions must renew credentials, and I believe it is important for professional genealogists to do so as well.

- BCG – Yes and we do renew every 5 years. This is one of the requirements that has recently changed, however. Renewal has been very easy for the past 3 times that I've renewed. The next time I renew I have to submit a proof argument, which has not been required before. I'm not sure why this change was instituted and it has caused me to have to take some classes to find out what the heck they're talking about because I don't take clients and don't write proof arguments. So maybe that was their point after all.

- BCG / ICAPGen – Yes, and I have to renew both of mine every five years.

- In France, our credentials are renewed every year with a new one-year professional card. At the same time a control [check] of our criminal record is made.

- AGRA – Yes, members should have to submit samples of work every 5 years and also maintain CPD logs.

- AGRA – Definitely, say every five years and demonstrate Continuing Professional Development.

- ASGRA – I think it is unrealistic to demand renewal of credentials, as long as performance is monitored informally. It is probably more effective to encourage training days and CPD, whether formal or informal – that way the maintenance of performance is manageable. All researchers evolve, just as new drivers evolve over the years, and it is unfair to discriminate against older (and usually more experienced) researchers just because they have not pursued a university course, or because they are over (or under) a certain age.

- AAGRA – No. Most conscientious professionals would keep up their knowledge through constant fresh reading, etc. as a matter of course. I completed a six-year apprenticeship in the 1950's. I am still learning!

- AGI – No, but I do think that more stringent CPD should be embarked upon.

9) **How do you think the relevant organisation(s) could make the attaining of professional credentials more attractive?**

- From AGI's point of view, we are already engaging with those that might think we are elitist through our Affiliate Programme. Possibilities of group insurance; special offers for members for data websites, etc.

- 1. More members; 2. through working with archives to ensure that AGRA members are recommended by archivitsts to do work for readers.

- AGRA - Benefits of membership, raising the profile of the organisations and pro-active dialogue with other bodies.

- AAGRA - Perhaps through the introduction of post-nominals, as it would mutely indicate the professionalism of the member.[93]

- In France, in the case of our chamber we have been more than satisfied on how it is run and cannot think of any way they could make it more attractive to become a member.

- BCG – I'm not sure. I think there are always going to be detractors because there are people that have been doing genealogy research for others for years who don't have credentials and don't feel they need them. There are many who feel that credentialed professionals are elitist and that's a stigma that's hard to ignore or fight.

- I think that organizations could make the advantages more apparent through better marketing and public awareness of the application procedures and benefits of attaining the credentials. BCG is taking a step forward in this direction with their new webinar series. For example, the webinar by Judy Russell helped reduce some of the anxiety some people felt about completing the Kinship Determination Project that is part of a BCG portfolio. When people better understand the requirements, the credential feels more attainable.

- BCG / ICAPGen – It's a limited audience at best. I think those that are interested currently seek it out. I think the current situation will remain until genealogy is recognized as a legitimate course of study at the University level and the education programs move toward

---

[93] AAGRA has since introduced post-nominal initials.

qualifying graduates to pass the requirements for the certifying bodies in much the same way as it is for any other organization in industry. Most disciplines have credentialing bodies – why wouldn't genealogists?

- ASGRA – I don't think it is a case of offering social networking in all its forms, which seems to be the modern approach. In certain cases, this is taking the place of accreditation, and is being demanded as a basic rather than an extra. Education is the way. While it is true that anyone can set up a genealogy research practice, the success of that practice does not depend on the person's ability to do genealogy research – it depends on their ability to run a business professionally and effectively. A good accrediting body should help their members with that side of things. It is an area sadly lacking in all the university and college courses on offer at present. After all, a professional genealogist is trying to make a living, not have a lively social life.

10) **How do you think the relevant organisation(s) could make the application process more attractive?**

- The webinar series makes the application process seem more approachable. BCG takes other steps, such as making sample portfolios available at conferences. Some other possibilities that might be considered would be to allow candidates to re-do only parts of the portfolio, if the problems were limited to only certain projects rather than being pervasive. Another option might be to consider charging less for second application, in order to encourage people who did not attain certification the first time to try again.

- I like the way that BCG approaches this. At conferences they make well-prepared successful applications available for review within the booth space of BCG for 30 minutes by those interested. They have to check them out and return them. This has been very popular and helps to demystify the process.

- The application process has been heavily worked on by ICAPGen to address this very issue. You can now complete your accreditation in "bite-sized" chunks and monitor your progress to completion. BCG uses an "on the clock" marketing strategy that appeals to a number of people – it lets others know that you are currently deep into completing your application and that it has a specific deadline. Currently, I think both of these have helped to increase the appeal to non-credentialed genealogists.

- Simplified guidance notes and application process; AGRA also has the Associate Member scheme and regular study days.

- ASGRA – There is nothing attractive about an application process, and it is irrelevant to the applicant. The process has (I hope) in most cases been thoroughly and carefully thought out. The accreditation is worth having and therefore needs to be endured.

- AAGRA – By attractive and informative web sites showing the necessity of professional help to the competent amateur researcher.

11) **More detailed observations would be welcome – feel free to elaborate as much as you wish.**

- In France the situation for professional genealogists is a bit different than the rest of the world as you are required to be part of a professional chamber, which in turn is part of the French national chamber [now Généalogistes de France] to be able to carry out our work. So in this respect our credential is compulsory and it is just therefore a question of which chamber to choose from (as there are several in France). Though most of them will be run the same way as [ours] in term of eligibility and obtaining of credentials.

- Thank you for writing about this subject and offering people the opportunity to provide input.

- BCG / ICAPGen – It would be nice to have a single credentialing organization that is either recognized in the US or for that matter, internationally. More open minds will have to work toward this goal.

- BCG / ICAPGen – Better marketing around what credential is right for you. For example, if you are going into library or archive reference, then the ICAPGen exam probably suits your needs better. If you are looking to do significant published client work in descendant format, then BCG is probably better, but both cover the discipline.

- BCG / ICAPGen – The credentialing organizations need to come into the twenty-first century and increase the electronic and application skills of the professional. This is either with a demonstrated personal skill set or an established network of staff that have those skills. A professional who manages an operation need not have all the skills themselves, but they should demonstrate that they have the resources to provide those solutions for their clients who desire it.

- AGRA – The real threat to professionals are the organisations that offer no membership criteria yet advertise themselves as a professional organisation.

- AAGRA – In this "Age of the Internet", researchers need professional guidance more than ever before. Because of the Internet many think it is "family tree made easy", being wooed by what spurious "facts" others have locked into the Internet, or are researching "by indexes" without reference or cross-reference to primary sources. I also believe so-called "expert" speakers at functions should use fresh material and an even fresher approach in speaking. Many are sick of the same old tired "breaking down brick walls" style.

- AAGRA – From a somewhat sceptical person re certain qualifications, I have come to see the need and necessity for such, not only for the advantages recognised credentials give your work and advice, but also for the satisfaction clients receive, knowing their problems are being handled by one who has the qualified knowledge and trust of the organisation behind them.

There were some surprising responses to both questionnaires. For instance, eight of the ten genealogists without credentials indicated that they had contemplated applying for accreditation. On the other hand six of them stated that they saw no need for credentials. None of the ten saw the application requirements as unattainable. This should not be surprising, as they all are experienced genealogists.

Renewal of credentials applies only to those granted by BCG and ICAPGen, which are irrelevant to most of the respondents. However, only two of the non-accredited genealogists indicated an aversion to the renewal criteria as a factor in their not applying for credentials, but one suggested that relaxing the renewal requirements would make the application process more attractive. Of the accredited genealogists, those with the BCG and ICAPGen credentials were in favour of the renewal criteria, but so also were two AGRA Members.

It is not surprising at all that the two non-accredited genealogists living outside the English-speaking areas of the world commented on the disadvantages of geographical location and language for people in their situation. Another person commented that BCG had no Canadian judging Canadian applications.

One of the ten on either side of the fence commented on the division between those with and without professional credentials. Both responses were from the USA, so perhaps it is more of an issue in that region.

'The attitude of many that have credentials seems to be that no one else is capable of doing the work without giving the individual a chance to prove they can.'
V.
'There are many who feel that credentialed professionals are elitist and that's a stigma that's hard to ignore or fight.'

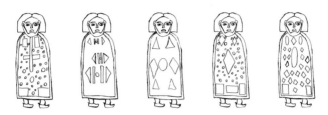

Some Personal Observations

I hope that this book will draw the attention of practitioners and aspiring practitioners to accrediting bodies and make them consider the benefits they bring to the profession. I hope too that it will make the accrediting bodies look at the practices of similar organisations in other regions and possibly learn from their example.

Having researched the subject of professional credentials over the past few years I have formed opinions on how accrediting organisations and others can improve the situation all round, for the benefit of the public and all true professional genealogists. Here, briefly, are my observations and ideas.

The accrediting bodies are generally run on a voluntary basis by working genealogists. For that reason it is understandable that their human resources are finite. While acknowledging such limitations, I believe that they could do more to make professional credentials widely known. Unless potential clients are aware of these credentials and what they mean, unless they know of the accrediting organisations, they are not going to seek out genealogists with a stamp of approval. All the hard work of the accrediting bodies is wasted if they are not actively putting themselves before the public.

In researching this subject I had occasion to contact most, but not all, of the accrediting bodies. To begin at a very basic level, one or two of these organisations (very much the minority) could improve their image by ensuring that email enquiries receive timely and professional responses. As already suggested, some could do more to make the general public aware of their very existence. Static websites with old information do little to promote professional credentials in general or the services of those accredited. Investing time and effort in a user-friendly website is essential. Having an active 'News' page is important. Naming other accrediting bodies on the 'Links' page is an important way of supporting professional credentials worldwide.

Also, having an active presence on social media now is almost *de rigueur* for any representative or accrediting organisation. It is also a relatively easy way to develop a profile for the organisation. Issuing press releases to key genealogical media people and to other accrediting bodies should be standard practice. I have noted, for example, that new categories of membership have been introduced by some organisations but the fact has not been communicated to the world. Applicants will be attracted to those categories only if they are told about them!

Co-operation between accrediting bodies is something that should develop if professional credentials are to receive the recognition they deserve. In this regard, ASGRA is a shining light. In recent years it has had a partnership with AGRA and it currently has an alliance with AGI. In a less public way there has been contact between representatives of a number of these organisations. Mutual support and sharing of ideas can only benefit the profession all round.

Promoting the services of members / those accredited is one important function of the accrediting bodies, but other forms of support are worth the effort. CPD is an important way of keeping credentials relevant. Some of the accrediting bodies have made great strides with this aspect and all would benefit from such developments. AAGRA has a major obstacle in this regard because of the vast geographical area it covers, but it already has embraced modern technology in relation to its annual general meeting, holding it by teleconference. Webinars could allow AAGRA hold virtual CPD sessions, as well as allowing various accrediting bodies hold virtual joint meetings.

All accrediting organisations could benefit from regularly reviewing all aspects of the accreditation they offer – for example, the application procedure, whether it is positively presented to potential applicants, the duration of credentials and the role of CPD in keeping the credentials relevant. A number of accrediting bodies have found ways of accommodating academic courses by offering those with certificates, diplomas or degrees recognition of their achievements when it comes to applying for professional credentials. In practical terms the requirements for such applicants are reduced. This arrangement is an acknowledgement of the growing importance of such courses as well as being mutually beneficial to those accrediting bodies and the course providers. However, there is a danger that these accrediting bodies may end up merely 'rubber-stamping' academic results instead of maintaining their own standards.

Education provides a certain level of technical knowledge. Experience develops that into true expertise.

- Donn Devine, 'Defining Professionalism', Professional Genealogy: a Manual for Researchers, Writers, Editors, Lecturers and Librarians, (Baltimore, Maryland 2001)

Quoted elsewhere in this book, BCG drew a distinction between academic qualifications and professional credentials, stating that the latter are 'a separate matter whose function is performed by boards or bars that are independent of teaching institutions'. Credentials confirm the acquisition of expertise through experience. Entirely substituting an academic qualification for experience ultimately will dilute the value of the credentials.

This is something that those behind the 'Register of Qualified Genealogists' (RQG) fail to appreciate, or possibly choose to ignore. Launched as recently as 2016, the RQG is an online register, not only of people who hold qualifications from certain British institutions, but also those who are studying for the same. It is not an accrediting body as it does not itself examine applicants' knowledge, skill or experience. It, therefore, fulfils the role of a support group and marketing agency for an exclusive subset of practitioners.

In my opinion, those responsible for setting up the RQG have demonstrated a total disregard for the work and value of the accrediting bodies in the British Isles. The disdain and disrespect shown to existing practitioners by the main instigator of the RQG, Bruce Durie, as outlined in SECTION 2, is difficult to ignore. Durie is now the 'RQG Ambassador', which suggests that the belligerent personal views he expressed a few years ago coincide with RQG policy.[94] This gives the impression that the RQG is attempting to usurp the role of the accrediting bodies and exclude from the profession all but those with certain academic qualifications. Of course, those academic course graduates who have subscribed to the RQG are not responsible for this state of affairs and, possibly, are unaware of the damaging effects of the Register. Indeed some of them also hold credentials as genealogists.

On the subjects of usurpation and exclusion, the Council for the Advancement of Forensic Genealogy (CAFG) appears to regard itself as the ultimate superstructure in accreditation in the USA. This is inferred from the fact that the holding of the Accredited Genealogist or Certified Genealogist credential merely admits a practitioner to CAFG's entry level, 'Peer Mentor Program'. Admittedly CAFG has identified a specialty field for itself. For this specialty it deems it necessary to progress through four preparatory stages before reaching the state of enlightenment that is the FCG credential. However, this smacks of an attempt to please an external entity (in this case the US legal system). In this attempt, CAFG is belittling and damaging the long-established AG and CG credentials.

Though CAFG has chosen to define legal genealogical research as 'forensic genealogy', it has specifically excluded traditional heir searchers from the fold, casting aspersions on their integrity as a class. Perhaps those earnest people who created CAFG might have done some good for the profession by investing their energies in bolstering the existing accrediting bodies in their country, while at the same time forming an organisation offering guidance in the legal aspects of the specialty.

Regarding language barriers, it is very important for genealogists who are not fluent in English or French to have access to professional credentials. It is by no means ideal to have an external organisation, unfamiliar with a region, its record keeping and its language, remotely conferring credentials. Unfortunately, genealogists in many areas of the world have to settle for that for now. It is very welcome news that *Verband deutschsprachiger Berufsgenealogen* is working towards accreditation. Having an accrediting organisation for German-speaking professionals would be a significant step in the right direction.

It should be remembered that most of the existing accrediting bodies came into being by the efforts of practitioners. They were not imposed from on

---

[94] RQG, 'Corporate Information', www.qualifiedgenealogists.org/corporate-information, accessed 18 July 2018.

SECTION 5 - SOME PERSONAL OBSERVATIONS

high. How I would see the establishment of accrediting systems is as follows. A group of genealogists organise a meeting or teleconference, inviting all known professionals to partake; some guidelines are agreed and possibly the help of an established national or international general membership society or another accrediting body is sought; a further meeting approves a set of rules; an independent board of assessors is appointed; all genealogists seeking professional credentials (including the founders) apply for accreditation. In my opinion, having an independent board of assessors is a very important element.

Spanish being one of the leading world languages, it should be possible to establish an accrediting organisation for Spanish-speaking genealogists, maybe even incorporating both Spain and Central / (most of) South America. It might be more difficult to create a similar accrediting body in parts of central and eastern Europe because of lower numbers of professionals speaking the same language. However, Poland is one country that has a significant number of genealogical firms and individual practitioners. Currently there is no support / networking organisation in Poland but perhaps this situation may change. If Polish professional genealogists were to establish an organisation they would be best advised to go all out and create an accrediting body rather than merely a support / networking group.[95]

It is not necessary to have a large number of practitioners in a linguistic region in order to start a credential system. If there are no more than about ten or twenty practising genealogists in a region there is no reason why a properly constituted accrediting organisation could not function. Co-operation between accrediting bodies could support smaller organisations in their efforts.

That is something there is not enough of: co-operation between accrediting bodies! It would seem like a sensible idea, but it does not happen in general. ASGRA, the Scottish accrediting organisation, has had a partnership with AGRA, representing England and Wales, while it is currently in an alliance with AGI, the Irish body, of which I am a member. That is the extent of official co-operation between the eight existing organisations. My personal experience of the alliance between ASGRA and AGI is a very positive one. The two bodies do not have identical criteria for membership or identical assessment processes, but they accept and respect the differences and they have much common ground. There has been some communication between AGI and AGRA, and between AGI and AAGRA, the Australasian body. I see co-operation between the accrediting

[95] I am grateful to Alan Jakman, editor of *More Maiorum*, for an insight into the situation in Poland.

129

bodies as important. As there are many more non-accredited than accredited genealogists in the world, it makes sense that those providing credentials should seek common ground in order to protect the profession.

Other organisations for professional genealogists could do more to bolster credentials within the field. The Association of Professional Genealogists has over 2,000 members, most of whom are unaccredited. In the past decade its membership outside North America has grown. Until recent years its website gave the impression that professional credentials were only those granted by BCG and ICAPGen. Now it refers to 'major genealogical testing programs' which 'include' BCG and ICAPGen.[96] This goes some way towards recognising the other international accrediting organisations.

In another section of the website APG lists 'Professional Genealogical Organizations' and 'International Genealogical Organizations', including almost all the international accrediting bodies. Unfortunately the two lists mix together accrediting bodies, support / networking organisations and a selection of general membership societies.[97] This is unfortunate, given that APG is in a strong position to advise its members and the general public about professional credentials specifically and about the accrediting bodies providing them throughout the world.

The only requirements for joining APG are the payment of the annual fee and a commitment to abide by its Code of Ethics. Theoretically anyone may join. This policy appears to be the cause of its rapid growth, out of proportion with accrediting organisations: a policy that may attract members for all the wrong reasons. I would question how this policy balances with the organisation's claim to be a professional association. Undoubtedly a large segment of its membership is comprised of untested and inexperienced aspiring professionals. It is only to be expected that at least some of those individuals lack the basic skills of the genealogist and that their lack of competence will damage the profession.

It would seem that such problems have been recognised for quite some time within APG. In the recently published *Professional Genealogy: Preparation, Practice & Standards*, Thomas W. Jones quoted concerns expressed by senior APG members, in one case as early as 1993, around the topic of open membership. One of those senior members was Jones himself. In 2007 he wrote:

> ... *APG's leaders could improve the field's professional standing. They could decide that*

[96] APG, 'Becoming a Professional', www.apgen.org/articles/ready.html, accessed 18 July 2018.
[97] APG, 'Resources for Professionals', www.apgen.org/resources/index.html, accessed 18 July 2018.

APG represents practitioners whose work meets professional standards. They could give priority to advancing the profession over meeting [members'] personal needs.[98]

In my opinion, APG would do more for the profession by concentrating on supporting the various accrediting organisations rather than simply growing its membership. Quality rather than quantity would be a good motto.

Finally, there is a major group of people who could and should make professional credentials much better known with the general public. These are the people who hold the credentials themselves. It is important for an accredited genealogist to highlight their professional credentials on their stationery, their websites and their social media outlets, to stipulate that their credentials be acknowledged when agreeing to lecture or when publishing articles, and to wear their accrediting organisation's pin (assuming there is one) at appropriate functions.

Many accredited genealogists do all these things. However, others, having gained the stamp of approval, do little to promote 'the brand' or to help run the organisation that has given them recognition. Those who have achieved professional credentials within genealogy should do all they can to highlight accreditation and to explain its worth. In the long run they are helping themselves. What goes around comes around.

[98] Thomas W. Jones, 'Are We Professionals? What APG Could Learn from Other Associations', *APG Quarterly*, December 2007, 173-177, quoted in Jones, 'Defining Professionalism', in Mills, *Professional Genealogy* (2018), 40-41.

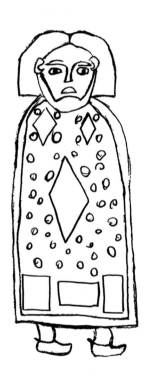

APPENDIX A

Educational Opportunities for All

Educational opportunities are for all, not just those who wish to become expert 'career amateurs' or accredited professionals. If you are a novice hobbyist you need to learn how to develop your knowledge and skills so that you can get the most enjoyment out of your hobby. It goes without saying that the more serious genealogy-enthusiast wants to learn the finer points.

As already mentioned, with the huge increase of interest in genealogy over the past decades the opportunity to learn from a mentor is very rare. Trial and error is a slow way of learning the ropes. Reading guide-books and getting in contact with more experienced researchers by joining a general membership society are good early steps, while attending lectures or studying a course would probably accelerate the learning process beyond the initial steps.

Guide-books on how to research family history are plentiful in relation to many geographical regions and ethnic or cultural groups. Books in relation to research skills, citation and developing a career in genealogy are rarer. The BIBLIOGRAPHY lists a selection of these. Perhaps the most widely known and influential is *ProGen* (*Professional Genealogy: a Manual for Researchers, Writers, Editors, Lecturers and Librarians*). It will be superseded quite rapidly by a newer version, *ProGen PPS*, which was published recently.

For those unfamiliar with general membership societies, APPENDIX B should give some initial pointers.

There are courses available in many parts of the world, as well as online. Some are basic, some advanced: many are for straightforward learning, while others offer academic credits or qualifications. The most important thing about all of them is that the genealogy-enthusiast should gain knowledge about the subject, regardless of how they may intend to employ it.

All such courses are not uniformly instructive. As mentioned earlier, anecdotal evidence suggests that standards vary. Undoubtedly there are some excellent courses at various levels. The lists below relate to known prominent courses on genealogy or related subjects currently on offer. They are by no means exhaustive. There are many more low-key offerings. Local libraries are a good place to enquire about availability. The following are listed for information purposes and no comment is offered as to their respective merits.

SHORT COURSES / 'INSTITUTES'

England

University of Oxford Department for Continuing Education [Oxford]
www.conted.ox.ac.uk/courses/what-is-local-history
· What is Local History?

France

Université de Nîmes [Nîmes]
https://www.unimes.fr/fr/formations/formation-continue/informations-sur-les-du/du-genealogiste-professionnelle.html
• *Diplôme Universitaire: Installation du généalogiste professionnel*

Northern Ireland

Irish Genealogy Essentials [Belfast; run by the Ulster Historical Foundation]
· www.ancestryireland.com/irish-genealogy-essentials

USA

British Institute [Salt Lake City, Utah; run by the International Society for British Genealogy and Family History]
· https://isbgfh.org

Genealogical Research Institute of Pittsburgh [Pittsburgh, Pennsylvania]
· www.gripitt.org

Gen-Fed (Genealogical Institute on Federal Records) [Washington, DC; formerly the National Institute on Genealogical Research]
· www.gen-fed.org/home/about-gen-fed

Institute of Genealogy and Historical Research [Athens, Georgia; formerly at Samford University, Alabama]
· http://ighr.gagensociety.org

Midwest African American Genealogy Institute [Fort Wayne, Indiana]
· www.maagiinstitute.org

Salt Lake Institute of Genealogy (SLIG) [Salt Lake City, Utah]
- http://slig.ugagenealogy.org

Salt Lake Institute of Genealogy (SLIG)
Academy for Professionals [Salt Lake City, Utah]
- http://slig.ugagenealogy.org

Salt Lake Institute of Genealogy (SLIG) Virtual [online]
- http://slig.ugagenealogy.org

Virtual Institute of Genealogical Research [online]
- http://vigrgenealogy.com

DISTANCE LEARNING:
ONLINE OR CORRESPONDENCE COURSES
English Language

Boston University Center for Professional Education [based in Boston, Massachusetts, USA]
  http://professional.bu.edu/programs/genealogy ;
  https://genealogyonline.bu.edu
  - Genealogical Research Certificate Program
  - Genealogical Principles Course

Brigham Young University–Idaho [based in Rexburg, Idaho, USA]
  www.byui.edu/online/degrees-and-programs
  - AAS in Family History Research
  - Certificate in Family History Research

City Colleges [based in Dublin, Ireland]
  www.citycolleges.ie/wp/diploma-family-history-genealogy
  - Diploma in Family History

Excelsior College Center for Professional Development [based in Albany, New York, USA]
  https://genealogy.excelsior.edu
  - Introduction to Genetic Genealogy
  - Advanced Genealogical Research

Family Tree University [run by Family Tree Magazine, based in Cincinnati, Ohio, USA]
> www.familytreeuniversity.com
> - a wide range of 4-week courses on subjects such as researching various ethnic origins, using various software packages, understanding DNA results, etc.

Institute of Heraldic and Genealogical Studies [based in Canterbury, England]
> www.ihgs.ac.uk/courses
> - Licentiateship
> - Diploma in Genealogy
> - Higher Certificate in Genealogy
> - IHGS Correspondence Course in Genealogy
> - Completing Your Ancestral Journey Correspondence Course
> - Broadening Your Family Tree Correspondence Course
> - Awaken Your Ancestors Correspondence Course
> - Heraldry Online Course
> - Tracing Your British Ancestors from Overseas

National Genealogical Society [based in Washington, DC, USA]
> www.ngsgenealogy.org/cs/educational_courses
> - American Genealogical Studies (4 courses available)
> - Continuing Genealogical Studies (9 courses available)
> - Family History Skills

National Institute for Genealogical Studies [based in Ontario, Canada]
> www.genealogicalstudies.com
> - Professional Learning Certificate in Genealogical Studies (relating to records of any of 7 geographical regions or methodology, librarianship or professional development)
> - Basic / Intermediate / Advanced Certificates

Pharos [based in Eastbourne, England]
> www.pharostutors.com
> - Family History Skills & Strategies (Advanced) Certificate Course
> - Family History Skills & Strategies (Intermediate) Certificate Course

- Tutor-Led Courses

- Anytime Courses

(both Family History Skills & Strategies courses are run in conjunction with the Society of Genealogists)

Saskatchewan Genealogical Society [based in Regina, Saskatchewan, Canada]
www.saskgenealogy.com/index.php/education/certification-courses
- Instructors Certification Course

- Aboriginal Researcher Certification Course

- Saskatchewan Researcher Certification Course

- Saskatchewan Record Searcher Certification Course

Society of Australian Genealogists [based in Sydney, New South Wales, Australia]
www.sag.org.au/events/courses-in-genealogy.html
- Diploma in Family Historical Studies

- Certificate in Genealogical Studies

Society of Genealogists [based in London, England]
www.sog.org.uk
(see Pharos, above)

University of Dundee Centre for Archive and Information Studies [based in Dundee, Scotland]
www.dundee.ac.uk/cais/
- Masters (MLitt) in Family and Local History

- Post-Graduate Diploma in Family and Local History

- Post-Graduate Certificate in Family and Local History

- Taster Courses in Family and Local History

University of Limerick Graduate School [based in Limerick, Ireland]
www.ul.ie/graduateschool/course/history-family-online-ma
www.ul.ie/ULH/certificate-programmes
- History of Family (Online) MA

- Certificate in History of Family and Genealogical Methods (with Irish Ancestry Research Centre)

University of New England [based in Armidale, New South Wales, Australia]
https://my.une.edu.au/courses/2017/courses/GDLFAH
- Graduate Diploma in Local, Family and Applied History

University of Oxford Department for Continuing Education [based in Oxford, England]
www.conted.ox.ac.uk/about/undergraduate-advanced-diploma-in-local-history
- Undergraduate Advanced Diploma in Local History (Online)

University of Strathclyde Centre for Lifelong Learning [based in Glasgow, Scotland]
www.strath.ac.uk/studywithus/centreforlifelonglearning/genealogy
- MSc in Genealogical, Palaeographic & Heraldic Studies
- Post-Graduate Diploma in Genealogical, Palaeographic & Heraldic Studies
- Post-Graduate Certificate in Genealogical, Palaeographic & Heraldic Studies
- Online Beginner to Intermediate Level Genealogy

University of Tasmania [based in Tasmania, Australia]
www.utas.edu.au/arts/diploma-of-family-history
- Diploma of Family History

French Language

Université de Nîmes [based in Nîmes, France]
www.unimes.fr/fr/formations/formation-continue/informations-sur-les-du/du-genealogie-histoire-des-familles.html
- *Diplôme Universitaire: Généalogie et histoire des familles* [38 hour course over one week]

Université du Maine [based in Le Mans, France]
http://formations-ead.univ-lemans.fr/du-genealogie/fr/index.html
- *Diplôme Universitaire: Histoire et généalogie familiale*

Spanish Language

HISPAGEN, *Asociación de Genealogía Hispana* [based in Madrid, Spain]
http://hispagen.es/index.php/curso-hispagen
· *Curso de Fundamentos de genealogía española*

Universidad Nacional de Educación a Distancia [National Distance Education University; based in Spain]
www.fundacion.uned.es/ http://www2.uned.es/master-der-nobiliario/
· *Master en Derecho Nobiliario y Premial, Heráldica y Genealogía*

· *Diploma de Especialista en Genealogía*

· *Diploma de Experto en Heráldica, Genealogía y Nobiliaria*

· *Diploma de Experto en Fuentes Genealógicas y Emblemáticas, Archivística y Documentación*

ON-SITE COURSES

England

University of Cambridge Institute of Continuing Education
www.ice.cam.ac.uk/courses/courses-subject/local-and-regional-history
· Undergraduate Diploma in Local History

· Undergraduate Certificate in Local History

University of Leicester Centre for English Local History
www2.le.ac.uk/centres/elh/postgraduate
· Research Degrees (MPhil / PhD)

· MA in English Local History and Family History

University of Oxford Department for Continuing Education [Oxford]
www.conted.ox.ac.uk/about/dphil-in-english-local-history
www.conted.ox.ac.uk/about/msc-in-english-local-history
· DPhil in English Local History

· MSc in English Local History

France

Université de Nîmes [Nîmes]

www.unimes.fr/fr/formations/formation-continue/informations-sur-les-du/du-genealogie-histoire-des-familles.html
- *Diplôme Universitaire: Généalogie et histoire des familles*

https://www.unimes.fr/fr/formations/formation-continue/informations-sur-les-du/du-genealogiste-professionnelle.html
- *Diplôme Universitaire: Installation du généalogiste professionnel*

Ireland (Republic of)

City Colleges [Dublin]

www.citycolleges.ie/wp/diploma-family-history-genealogy
- Diploma in Family History

University College Cork Adult Continuing Education [Cork, Ireland]

www.ucc.ie/en/ace-dgnl
- Diploma in Genealogy (with Irish Ancestry Research Centre)

University of Limerick [Limerick, Ireland]

www.ul.ie/graduateschool/course/history-family-ma
www.ul.ie/ULH/certificate-programmes
- History of Family MA

- Certificate in History of Family and Genealogical Methods (with Irish Ancestry Research Centre)

Scotland

University of Strathclyde Centre for Lifelong Learning [Glasgow]

www.strath.ac.uk/studywithus/centreforlifelonglearning/genealogy
- On-Campus Beginner to Intermediate Level Genealogy

Spain

Asociación de Diplomados en Genealogía, Heráldica y Nobiliaria [Madrid]

www.adghn.org/index.php/cursos
- Courses on genealogy and related subjects

USA

Brigham Young University [Provo, Utah]
https://home.byu.edu/home
- BA in Family History / Genealogy

Wales

Aberystwyth University
www.aber.ac.uk/en/lifelong-learning/genealogy/
- Certificate in Genealogical Studies

N o law graduate comes out a solicitor; no medicine graduate comes out a doctor; no accountancy graduate comes out an accountant. Further training and experience is required to make them professional.

- Janet Bishop, Member of ASGRA & AGRA[99]

---

[99] Janet Bishop, 'When a vocation calls', www.angliaresearch.co.uk/articles/when-a-vocation-calls, accessed 18 July 2018.

Federations & General Membership Genealogical Organisations

It will be useful for those developing a career in genealogy to identify relevant organisations that may afford them educational opportunities and a circle of colleagues. Such organisations are particularly important for aspiring professionals in geographical or linguistic areas where there are no relevant professional credentials. Also, there are several societies based in the USA that specialise in areas of Europe. The following lists may be of assistance.

The first list is of federations of membership societies. Generally they are not open for individuals to join, but their lists of constituent organisations may be of help, particularly in relation to smaller regional societies.

FEDERATIONS

Association of Family History Societies of Wales
www.fhswales.org.uk

Australasian Federation of Family History Organisations
www.affho.org

Council of Irish Genealogical Organisations
www.cigo.ie

Deutschen Arbeitsgemeinschaft genealogischer Verbände e. V.
(Federation of German genealogical associations)
http://wiki-de.genealogy.net/DAGV

Fédération Française de Généalogie
www.genefede.eu

Federation of East European Family History Societies (USA)
www.feefhs.org

Federation of Family History Societies
www.ffhs.org.uk

Federation of Genealogical Societies
https://fgs.org

Fédération québécoise des sociétés de généalogie
http://federationgenealogie.qc.ca

International Association of Jewish Genealogical Societies
www.iajgs.org

International German Genealogy Partnership
https://iggpartner.org

Nordgen (Nordic countries)
www.nordgen.com

Scottish Association of Family History Societies
www.safhs.org.uk

Sveriges Släktforskarförbund
(Federation of Swedish Genealogical Societies)
www.genealogi.se/the-federation

The following are general membership organisations within genealogy, ones that anyone may join. The list is by no means comprehensive. It covers the larger or more significant or geographically important genealogical societies that are open to all.

Argentina

Asociación de Genealogía Judía de Argentina
www.agja.org.ar

Instituto Argentino de Ciencias Genealógicas (Argentina)
www.institutogenealogia.org

Australia

Australian Jewish Genealogical Society
www.ajgs.org.au

Genealogical Society of Queensland
www.gsq.org.au

Genealogical Society of Victoria
www.gsv.org.au

Queensland Family History Society
www.qfhs.org.au

Society of Australian Genealogists
www.sag.org.au

South Australian Genealogy & Heraldry Society
www.genealogysa.org.au

Tasmanian Family History Society
www.tasfhs.org

Victorian GUM [Genealogists Using Microcomputers]
www.vicgum.asn.au

Western Australian Genealogical Society
http://membership.wags.org.au

Austria

East European Genealogical Society (Canada)
www.eegsociety.org

Heraldisch-Genealogischen Gesellschaft "ADLER"
www.adler-wien.at

Hungarian Genealogical Society of Greater Cleveland (USA)
www.hungariangensocietycleveland.org

Österreichische Gesellschaft für Genealogie und Geschichte
www.familia-austria.at

Palatines to America German Genealogy Society
www.palam.org

Vereinigung Sudetendeutscher Familienforscher
www.genealogienetz.de/vereine/VSFF

Belarus

East European Genealogical Society (Canada)
www.eegsociety.org

Germans from Russia Heritage Society (USA)
www.grhs.org

Belgium

Familiekunde Vlaanderen
   www.familiekunde-vlaanderen.be

Bohemia

Czech & Slovak American Genealogy Society of Illinois (USA)
   www.csagsi.org

Czechoslovak Genealogical Society International
   www.cgsi.org

East European Genealogical Society (Canada)
   www.eegsociety.org

Vereinigung Sudetendeutscher Familienforscher
   www.genealogienetz.de/vereine/VSFF

Bosnia and Herzagovina

Hungarian Genealogical Society of Greater Cleveland (USA)
   www.hungariangensocietycleveland.org

Brazil

Colégio Brasileiro de Genealogia (Brazil)
   www.cbg.org.br

Canada

Alberta Family Histories Society
   www.afhs.ab.ca

Alberta Genealogical Society
   www.abgensoc.ca

American-Canadian Genealogical Society (USA)
   https://acgs.org

British Columbia Genealogical Society
   www.bcgs.ca

British Isles Family History Society of Greater Ottawa
   www.bifhsgo.ca

East European Genealogical Society
   www.eegsociety.org

Family History Society of Newfoundland and Labrador
www.fhsnl.ca

Genealogical Association of Nova Scotia
www.novascotiaancestors.ca

Manitoba Genealogical Society
www.mbgenealogy.com

New Brunswick Genealogical Society
www.nbgs.ca

Ontario Genealogical Society
www.ogs.on.ca

Prince Edward Island Genealogical Society
www.peigs.ca

Quebec Family History Society
www.qfhs.ca

Saskatchewan Genealogical Society
www.saskgenealogy.com

Société généalogique canadienne-française
www.sgcf.com

Society for German Genealogy in Eastern Europe
www.sggee.org

United Empire Loyalists' Association of Canada
www.uelac.org

Caribbean

Instituto Dominicano de Genealogía (Dominican Republic)
www.idg.org.do

Sociedad Puertorriqueña de Genealogía (Puerto Rica)
www.genealogiapr.com

Catholics

Catholic Family History Society (UK)
http://catholicfhs.online

Chile

Instituto Chileno de Investigaciones Genealógicas (Chile)
www.genealogia.cl

Computer Genealogy

DIS-Danmark (Denmark)
www.slaegtogdata.dk

DIS-Norge, Slekt og Data (Norway)
www.disnorge.no

Föreningen DIS (Sweden)
www.dis.se

Silicon Valley Computer Genealogy Group (USA)
www.svcgg.org

Victorian GUM [Genealogists Using Microcomputers] (Australia)
www.vicgum.asn.au

Croatia

Hungarian Genealogical Society of Greater Cleveland (USA)
www.hungariangensocietycleveland.org

Czech Republic

Czech & Slovak American Genealogy Society of Illinois (USA)
www.csagsi.org

Czechoslovak Genealogical Society International
www.cgsi.org

East European Genealogical Society (Canada)
www.eegsociety.org

Hungarian Genealogical Society of Greater Cleveland (USA)
www.hungariangensocietycleveland.org

Denmark

Danish American Heritage Society
www.danishheritage.org

DIS-Danmark
www.slaegtogdata.dk

Jødisk Genealogisk Selskab i Danmark
www.jgs-danmark.dk

National Danish-American Genealogical Society
www.danishgenealogy.org

Palatines to America German Genealogy Society
www.palam.org

Samfundet for Dansk Genealogi og Personalhistorie
www.genealogi.dk

England (see Great Britain)

Estonia

Eesti Genealoogia Seltsi
www.genealoogia.ee

Finland

Suomen Sukututkimusseura
www.genealogia.fi

Flemish

Familiekunde Vlaanderen
www.familiekunde-vlaanderen.be

France

Ancêtres Italiens
http://geneaita.org

Cercle de Généalogie Juive
www.genealoj.org

La France Généalogique
www.cegf.org

Genetics

International Society of Genetic Genealogists
https://isogg.org/

Germany

American Historical Society of Germans from Russia
www.ahsgr.org

Anglo-German Family History Society (UK)
www.agfhs.org

Arbeitsgemeinschaft für mitteldeutsche Familienforschung
www.amf-verein.de

East European Genealogical Society (Canada)
www.eegsociety.org

Germanic Genealogy Society (USA)
www.ggsmn.org

Germans from Russia Heritage Society (USA)
www.grhs.org

Herold
www.herold-verein.de

Palatines to America German Genealogy Society
www.palam.org

Society for German Genealogy in Eastern Europe (Canada)
www.sggee.org

Vereinigung Sudetendeutscher Familienforscher
www.genealogienetz.de/vereine/VSFF

Great Britain

Anglo-German Family History Society
www.agfhs.org

Anglo-Italian Family History Society
https://anglo-italianfhs.org.uk

British Isles Family History Society of Greater Ottawa
www.bifhsgo.ca

Catholic Family History Society
http://catholicfhs.online

Families in British India Society
www.fibis.org

Foundation for Medieval Genealogy
http://fmg.ac

Guild of One Name Studies
https://one-name.org

Huguenot Society of Great Britain & Ireland
www.huguenotsociety.org.uk

International Society for British Genealogy and Family History (USA)
https://isbgfh.org

Irish Genealogical Research Society
www.irishancestors.ie

Jewish Genealogical Society of Great Britain
www.jgsgb.org.uk

Quaker Family History Society
www.qfhs.co.uk

Romany & Traveller Family History Society
https://rtfhs.org.uk

Scottish Genealogy Society
www.scotsgenealogy.com

Society of Genealogists
www.sog.org.uk

Gypsy (see Romany)

Hispanic

Asociación de Genealogía Hispana (Spain)
www.hispagen.es

Genealogical Society of Hispanic America (USA)
www.gsha.net

Huguenot

Huguenot Society of America
www.huguenotsocietyofamerica.org

Huguenot Society of Great Britain & Ireland
www.huguenotsociety.org.uk

Huguenot Society of South Africa
www.hugenoot.org.za

Hungary

East European Genealogical Society (Canada)
www.eegsociety.org

Hungarian Genealogical Society of Greater Cleveland (USA)
www.hungariangensocietycleveland.org

Iceland

Ættfræðifélagið (Icelandic Genealogy Society)
http://aett.is

India

Families in British India Society
    www.fibis.org

International

The Augustan Society
    https://augustansociety.org

Foundation for Medieval Genealogy
    http://fmg.ac

Genealogical Speakers Guild
    www.genealogicalspeakersguild.org

Guild of One Name Studies
    https://one-name.org

International Society of Family History Writers and Editors
    www.isfhwe.org

International Society of Genetic Genealogy
    https://isogg.org

The Surname Society
    http://surname-society.org

Virtual Genealogical Association
    http://virtualgensoc.com

Ireland (see also Northern Ireland)

British Isles Family History Society of Greater Ottawa
    www.bifhsgo.ca

Huguenot Society of Great Britain & Ireland
    www.huguenotsociety.org.uk

International Society for British Genealogy and Family History (USA)
    https://isbgfh.org

Irish Genealogical Research Society
    www.irishancestors.ie

Irish Genealogical Society International (USA)
    https://irishgenealogical.org

Quaker Family History Society
    www.qfhs.co.uk

TIARA - The Irish Ancestral Research Association (USA)
https://tiara.ie

Italy

Ancêtres Italiens (France)
http://geneaita.org

Anglo-Italian Family History Society (UK)
https://anglo-italianfhs.org.uk

Italian Genealogical Group (USA)
www.italiangen.org

Israel

Israel Genealogical Society
www.isragen.org.il

Jewish

Asociación de Genealogía Judía de Argentina
www.agja.org.ar

Australian Jewish Genealogical Society
www.ajgs.org.au

Cercle de Généalogie Juive (France)
www.genealoj.org

East European Genealogical Society (Canada)
www.eegsociety.org

Israel Genealogical Society
www.isragen.org.il

Jewish Genealogical Society (USA)
www.jewishgen.org

Jewish Genealogical Society of Great Britain
www.jgsgb.org.uk

Jewish Genealogical Society of South Africa
www.facebook.com/JGSSA2017

Jødisk Genealogisk Selskab i Danmark (Denmark)
www.jgs-danmark.dk

Judiska Släktforskningsföreningen i Sverige (Sweden)
www.judgen.se

Nederlandse Kring voor Joodse Genealogie (Netherlands)
www.nljewgen.org

Schweizerische Vereinigung für Jüdische Genealogie (Switzerland)
www.svjg.ch

Liechtenstein

Palatines to America German Genealogy Society
www.palam.org

Lithuania

Lithuanian Global Genealogical Society (USA)
www.lithuaniangenealogy.org

Luxembourg

Palatines to America German Genealogy Society
www.palam.org

Moravia

Czech & Slovak American Genealogy Society of Illinois (USA)
www.csagsi.org

Czechoslovak Genealogical Society International
www.cgsi.org

East European Genealogical Society (Canada)
www.eegsociety.org

Moravian Heritage Society (USA)
www.czechusa.com

Vereinigung Sudetendeutscher Familienforscher
www.genealogienetz.de/vereine/VSFF

Netherlands

Nederlandse Genealogische Vereniging
www.ngv.nl

Nederlandse Kring voor Joodse Genealogie
www.nljewgen.org

Palatines to America German Genealogy Society
www.palam.org

New Zealand

New Zealand Society of Genealogists
www.genealogy.org.nz

Northern Ireland (see also Ireland)

North of Ireland Family History Society
www.nifhs.org

Norway

DIS-Norge, Slekt og Data
www.disnorge.no

Norsk Slektshistorisk Forening
www.genealogi.no

Norwegian-American Genealogical Association
www.norwegianamerican.org

One-Name

Guild of One Name Studies
https://one-name.org

The Surname Society
http://surname-society.org

Palatine

Palatines to America German Genealogy Society
www.palam.org

Peru

Instituto Peruano de Investigaciones Genealógicas (Peru)
www.genealogiaperu.org

Poland

American Historical Society of Germans from Russia
www.ahsgr.org

East European Genealogical Society (Canada)
www.eegsociety.org

Opolscy Genealodzy
https://genealodzy.opole.pl

Palatines to America German Genealogy Society
www.palam.org

Polish Genealogical Society of America
www.pgsa.org

Polish Genealogical Society of Minnesota (USA)
http://pgsmn.org

Polskie Towarzystwo Genealogiczne
https://genealodzy.pl

Śląskie Towarzystwo Genealogiczne
http://genealodzy.wroclaw.pl

Society for German Genealogy in Eastern Europe (Canada)
www.sggee.org

Towarzystwo Genealogiczne Centralnj Polski
http://tgcp.pl

Warszawskie Towarzystwo Genealogiczne
https://wtg.org.pl

Quakers

Quaker Family History Society (UK)
www.qfhs.co.uk

Romania

East European Genealogical Society (Canada)
www.eegsociety.org

Hungarian Genealogical Society of Greater Cleveland (USA)
www.hungariangensocietycleveland.org

Romanian Genealogical Society (USA)
http://romaniangenealogy.com

Romany

Romany & Traveller Family History Society (UK)
https://rtfhs.org.uk

Russia

American Historical Society of Germans from Russia
www.ahsgr.org

East European Genealogical Society (Canada)
www.eegsociety.org

Germans from Russia Heritage Society (USA)
    www.grhs.org

Society for German Genealogy in Eastern Europe (Canada)
    https://www.sggee.org

Scotland (see also Great Britain)

Scottish Genealogy Society
    www.scotsgenealogy.com

Serbia

Hungarian Genealogical Society of Greater Cleveland (USA)
    www.hungariangensocietycleveland.org

Slovakia

Czech & Slovak American Genealogy Society of Illinois (USA)
    www.csagsi.org

Czechoslovak Genealogical Society International
    www.cgsi.org

East European Genealogical Society (Canada)
    www.eegsociety.org

Hungarian Genealogical Society of Greater Cleveland (USA)
    www.hungariangensocietycleveland.org

South Africa

Genealogical Society of South Africa
    www.genza.org.za

Huguenot Society of South Africa
    www.hugenoot.org.za

Jewish Genealogical Society of South Africa
    www.facebook.com/JGSSA2017

Spain

Asociación de Genealogía Hispana
    www.hispagen.es

Surnames (see One-Name)

Sweden

Föreningen DIS
    www.dis.se

Genealogiska Föreningen
   www.genealogi.net

Judiska Släktforskningsföreningen i Sverige
   www.judgen.se

Sällskapet Vallonättlingar
   www.vallon.se

Svenska Genealogiska Samfundet
   www.genealogiska-samfundet.se

Swedish Genealogical Society of Minnesota
   www.sgsmn.org

Swenson Swedish Immigration Research Center (USA)
   www.augustana.net/general-information/swenson-center

Switzerland

Palatines to America German Genealogy Society
   www.palam.org

Schweizerische Gesellschaft für Familienforschung
   www.sgffweb.ch

Schweizerische Vereinigung für Jüdische Genealogie
   www.svjg.ch

Traveller

Romany & Traveller Family History Society (UK)
   https://rtfhs.org.uk

UK (see Great Britain; Northern Ireland; Scotland)

Ukraine

American Historical Society of Germans from Russia
   www.ahsgr.org

East European Genealogical Society (Canada)
   www.eegsociety.org

Germans from Russia Heritage Society (USA)
   www.grhs.org

Hungarian Genealogical Society of Greater Cleveland (USA)
   www.hungariangensocietycleveland.org

Palatines to America German Genealogy Society
   www.palam.org

Society for German Genealogy in Eastern Europe (Canada)
   www.sggee.org

Uruguay

Instituto de Estudios Genealógicos del Uruguay
   www.iegu.org.uy

USA

Afro-American Historical and Genealogical Society
   www.aahgs.org

Alabama Genealogical Society
   http://algensoc.org

American-Canadian Genealogical Society
   https://acgs.org

American Historical Society of Germans from Russia
   www.ahsgr.org

Arkansas Genealogical Society
   www.agsgenealogy.org

The Augustan Society
   https://augustansociety.org

California Genealogical Society
   www.californiaancestors.org

Colorado Genealogical Society
   www.cogensoc.us

Connecticut Society of Genealogists
   http://ctfamilyhistory.com

Czech & Slovak American Genealogy Society of Illinois
   www.csagsi.org

Czechoslovak Genealogical Society International
   www.cgsi.org

Danish American Heritage Society
   www.danishheritage.org

Delaware Genealogical Society
https://delgensoc.org

Family History Society of Arizona
www.fhsa.org

Florida State Genealogical Society
https://flsgs.org

Genealogical Society of Hispanic America
www.gsha.net

Genealogical Society of New Jersey
www.gsnj.org

Genealogical Society of Pennsylvania
https://genpa.org

Genealogical Society of Vermont
www.genealogyvermont.org

Genealogical Speakers Guild
www.genealogicalspeakersguild.org

Georgia Genealogical Society
www.gagensociety.org

Germanic Genealogy Society
www.ggsmn.org

Germans from Russia Heritage Society
www.grhs.org

Huguenot Society of America
www.huguenotsocietyofamerica.org

Hungarian Genealogical Society of Greater Cleveland (USA)
www.hungariangensocietycleveland.org

Idaho Genealogical Society
http://idahogenealogy.org

Illinois State Genealogical Society
https://ilgensoc.org

Indiana Genealogical Society
www.indgensoc.org

International Society for British Genealogy and Family History
https://isbgfh.org

International Society of Family History Writers and Editors
www.isfhwe.org

International Society of Genetic Genealogy
https://isogg.org

Irish Genealogical Society International
https://irishgenealogical.org

Italian Genealogical Group
www.italiangen.org

Jewish Genealogical Society
www.jewishgen.org

Lithuanian Global Genealogical Society
www.lithuaniangenealogy.org

Louisiana Genealogical & Historical Society
www.louisianaghs.org

Minnesota Genealogical Society
http://mngs.org

Missouri State Genealogical Association
https://mosga.org

Moravian Heritage Society
www.czechusa.com

National Danish-American Genealogical Society
www.danishgenealogy.org

National Genealogical Society
www.ngsgenealogy.org

Nebraska State Genealogical Society
https://nsgs.org

New England Historic Genealogical Society
www.americanancestors.org

New Mexico Genealogical Society
www.nmgs.org

New York Genealogical & Biographical Society
www.newyorkfamilyhistory.org

North Carolina Genealogical Society
www.ncgenealogy.org

Norwegian-American Genealogical Association
www.norwegianamerican.org

Ohio Genealogical Society
www.ogs.org

Oklahoma Genealogical Society
https://okgensoc.org

Palatines to America German Genealogy Society
www.palam.org

Polish Genealogical Society of America
www.pgsa.org

Polish Genealogical Society of Minnesota
http://pgsmn.org

Rhode Island Genealogical Society
https://rigensoc.org

Romanian Genealogical Society
http://romaniangenealogy.com

Southern California Genealogical Society
http://scgsgenealogy.com

Silicon Valley Computer Genealogy Group
www.svcgg.org

Swedish Genealogical Society of Minnesota
www.sgsmn.org

Swenson Swedish Immigration Research Center
www.augustana.net/general-information/swenson-center

Texas State Genealogical Society
www.txsgs.org

TIARA - The Irish Ancestral Research Association
https://tiara.ie

Utah Genealogical Association
www.infouga.org

Virginia Genealogical Society
www.vgs.org

Western Reserve Historical Society
www.wrhs.org

Wisconsin State Genealogical Society
https://wsgs.org

Wales (see Great Britain)

Walloon

Sällskapet Vallonättlingar (Sweden)
www.vallon.se

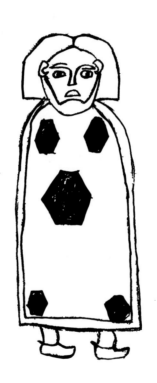

The Accrediting Bodies

The various accrediting bodies are the subject of this Appendix. It deals with their geographical coverage, codes of practice, complaints investigation facilities, credentials, honorific and non-credential categories, and post-nominal initials or terms, as well as explaining the process of obtaining a credential and its duration. This Appendix is followed by ancillary sections (C I-III) with details of other organisations related to accreditation.

ACCREDITED GENEALOGISTS IRELAND (AGI)

WEBSITE: http://accreditedgenealogists.ie

Overview

The organisation dates its existence from a meeting held in Belfast in May 1986. It was founded as the Association of Professional Genealogists in Ireland[100] (APGI). The name was changed in 2015 to Accredited Genealogists Ireland. In April 2016 it entered an alliance with ASGRA. The status of Fellow was introduced in 2004, followed by Affiliate in 2012 and Emeritus Member in 2015.

AGI is governed by a Council (including officers: President, Vice-President, Honorary Secretary, Honorary Treasurer) elected annually from within its membership. The officers may be re-elected for up to a maximum of three consecutive years. There is no time limit on ordinary Council members. The Council normally meets in Dublin. The annual general meeting is usually held in Dublin, but occasionally in Belfast instead.

Geographical Coverage

To obtain AGI credentials a genealogist must be resident on the island of Ireland (Republic of Ireland or Northern Ireland) and conducting all or most of his / her genealogical research in Irish records.

Code of Practice

Those admitted to membership of AGI must sign and abide by the organisation's Code of Practice [http://accreditedgenealogists.ie/constitution/#code]. Affiliates must abide by the Code of Practice, signing it when and if they become members.

Complaints Investigation

A complaint against a member is treated as confidential. Initially it is handled by the Honorary Secretary and President of AGI. If it cannot be resolved amicably, in consultation with the complainant and the member, in must go before the independent Complaints Investigation Panel. The panel has up to four members, none of whom is a Member of AGI. The chair-holder of the panel selects two panel members to assess each case. The final decision on each complaint rests with the chair-holder. Potentially the panel may recommend expulsion of the member in question.

---

[100] Originally Association of Professional Genealogists *of* Ireland.

Credential Categories

MEMBER: AGI accredits genealogists only. There is one credential category, that of Member. A Member must participate in CPD. A Member may be granted the status of Fellow (see below under 'Honorific Categories').

Honorific Categories

EMERITUS MEMBER: A Member or Associate Member may be granted the status of Emeritus Member on retirement from practice as a professional genealogist. The granting of the status is not automatic. An Emeritus Member holds the entitlements of associate membership (see below) for life.

FELLOW: A Member, Associate Member or former Member may be granted the status of Fellow in recognition of exceptional service to AGI or a particularly outstanding contribution to the study of Irish genealogy. A Fellow retains all the entitlements of membership for life.

Non-Credential Categories

AGI AFFILIATE: A reputable genealogist in the early stages of their transition to professional research may apply for AGI Affiliate status. They must meet the basic requirements of membership eligibility and apply by letter, with supporting documentation, and submit a dissertation or report of approximately 1,000 words. As an Affiliate is not accorded any level of accreditation their application is assessed by a sub-committee of AGI's Council. The number of Affiliates is limited at the discretion of the Council. Those admitted to Affiliate status are bound by AGI's Code of Practice and must partake in AGI's CPD programme. They are given a mentor and invited to all AGI events. They must apply for Member status within two years. If unsuccessful, they may remain Affiliates for a further two years before making a final membership application.

ASSOCIATE MEMBER: A Member who ceases to practice as a professional genealogist in Ireland or who takes up full-time employment outside of genealogy may not retain full membership. Instead they retain a link to AGI as an Associate Member for up to five years. They may resume full membership anytime within that period, if their circumstances change. Otherwise they cease to have any association with AGI.

Post-Nominal Initials or Terms

AGI Affiliate (denotes unaccredited Accredited Genealogists Ireland Affiliate)
FAGI (denotes Fellow of Accredited Genealogists Ireland)
MAGI (denotes Member of Accredited Genealogists Ireland)

Obtaining a Credential

MEMBER (MAGI)

To be eligible to apply for membership one must:

- have practised as a professional genealogist for not less than one year full-time or two years part-time.
- be resident in Ireland.
- be conducting all or most of one's genealogical research in Irish records.
- not be employed at any full-time occupation other than that of a professional genealogist.

What is involved in applying for Credentials

AN APPLICANT MUST

- submit a sample of work which should be a copy of a report already submitted to a client and completed no more than two years before the date of application; it should be a typescript report on research conducted over a period of 7 to 10 hours, exclusive of report preparation time.
- submit reproductions of the relevant photocopies or other documentation provided to the client.
- submit a letter stating that the sample of work is an accurate copy of the original report issued to the client and giving permission to AGI to contact the client should the need arise.
- submit a letter from the client giving permission for a copy of the original report to be provided to the assessors.
- (unless a current Affiliate) submit a reference form containing the names of three referees, one of whom must be a client who can attest to the applicant's satisfactory genealogical work, and the other two referees of standing who can vouch for the applicant's character and integrity.
- submit an application form.

· submit an application fee.

· (unless a current Affiliate) present for interview with two AGI officers.

Assessment Process

Membership applications are treated as confidential and the identity of the acting judges is not revealed. The Honorary Secretary of AGI passes each application to the chair-holder of the independent Board of Assessors. The board has up to ten members, who are archivists, librarians, retired genealogists, academic historians or others knowledgeable in the field of genealogical research. Members (and Fellows) of AGI are not eligible to serve on the board. The chair-holder selects three board members to assess each application. The chair-holder reports the board's decision to the Honorary Secretary of AGI, with observations on the applicant's work, which are passed to the applicant regardless of the board's decision. If the board approves the application it is put to the Council of AGI for ratification. The applicant must sign the AGI Code of Practice and pay the annual membership subscription on admission.

Duration of Credentials

Credentials are linked to membership of AGI. Members must participate in CPD and make quarterly CPD accounts. Membership is retained indefinitely, on payment of an annual fee, unless disqualification occurs for one of the following reasons:

· submission of a letter of resignation.

· expulsion on the recommendation of the Complaints Investigation Panel.

· ceasing to practice as a professional genealogist in Ireland.

· taking up full-time employment outside of genealogy.

AGI's constitution recognises that professional genealogists admitted to membership 'may apply their genealogical expertise primarily to consultancy or technology' and this does not disqualify them from retaining full membership. However, members who do not remain in Ireland or who take up full-time employment in another field are eligible only to remain as Associate Members. This status gives them no accreditation. They may remain as Associate Members for up to five years before resuming full membership, if they then fulfil the criteria. Otherwise they cease to have any association with AGI. Members conferred with the Fellowship of AGI are exempt from disqualification under the last two points.

ASSOCIATION OF GENEALOGISTS
AND RESEARCHERS IN ARCHIVES (AGRA)

WEBSITE: www.agra.org.uk

Overview

AGRA was formed in June 1968 as the Association of Genealogists and Record Agents. In 2001 the name changed to the Association of Genealogists and Researchers in Archives, but retained the acronym AGRA. In 2010 AGRA entered a formal partnership with ASGRA, which lasted to June 2017.

Initially membership was by invitation, based on reputation, but a formal application process soon evolved. In 1991 AGRA introduced the new category of Affiliate Member (now Associate) for those working towards gaining full membership. Since 1995 awards from the Institute of Heraldic and Genealogical Studies in Canterbury have been accepted as part of the entry requirements for membership, along with evidence of experience and professional acumen. In September 2014 the application criteria for Members and Associates changed, with new emphasis on genealogical courses and CPD. In June 2018 the emphasis on courses was expanded.

AGRA's current President is Patric L. Dickinson, Clarenceux King of Arms, and there are two Vice-Presidents. The President is an external individual, while the Vice-Presidents may be external or from within the membership. They are not part of AGRA's governing Council. The Council is presided over by a Chairman. To be eligible for the position of Chairman a Member must have served a minimum of 12 months on the Council. The Chairman is elected each year at the Annual General Meeting and may serve up to five consecutive years in the role. Ordinary Council members are elected at the Annual General Meeting (or may be co-opted if a vacancy arises) and serve a three-year term, with the option to serve a second term, to a maximum of six consecutive years. The Secretary and Treasurer are not Council members. They are appointed by Council and are not subject to a limited term of office. They may be AGRA Members or Associates or external individuals. The annual general meeting is held in London.

Geographical coverage

To obtain AGRA credentials a genealogist must be resident within the British Isles and involved in genealogical research using English or Welsh records as part of their profession.

Code of Practice

Those admitted as Members or Associates of AGRA must abide by the organisation's Code of Practice [www.agra.org.uk/about-code-of-practice].

Complaints Investigation

AGRA offers an arbitration service in case of a breakdown of relationship between a client and a Member or Associate of AGRA. It is stipulated that all parties should 'observe strict rules of confidentiality'.

Credential Categories

MEMBER: Though in the past AGRA differentiated between genealogists and researchers in archives, and had a category of specialist researcher, it now accredits genealogists only. There is one full credential category, that of Member. A Member may be granted the status of Fellow (see below under 'Honorific Categories').

ASSOCIATE: A genealogist working towards full membership may apply for partial credentials as an Associate of AGRA.

Honorific Categories

FELLOW: A Member may be granted the status of Fellow in recognition of service and contribution to AGRA or the profession of genealogy.

Post-Nominal Initials or Terms

AGRA (denotes membership of the Association of Genealogists and Researchers in Archives)

AGRA Associate / Associate of AGRA (denotes Associate of the Association of Genealogists and Researchers in Archives)

FGRA (denotes Fellow of the Association of Genealogists and Researchers in Archives)

Obtaining a Credential

MEMBER

To be eligible to apply for membership one must:

- be operating or intending to operate a genealogical research service using English or Welsh records and their work should include original sources and research prior to 1837.
- be resident in the British Isles.

What is involved in applying for Credentials

An applicant must:

- apply online through the AGRA website.
- submit an application fee.
- present for interview with the Board of Assessors, to include discussion of the applicant's research assignment and research reports: interviews are held twice yearly.

Additional criteria depend on the applicant's circumstance, as follows:

- holding the Diploma in Genealogy [DipGen] from the Institute of Heraldic and Genealogical Studies.[101]
- holding a Higher Certificate (or higher) from the Institute of Heraldic and Genealogical Studies, or a Post-Graduate Certificate in Genealogical, Palaeographic and Heraldic Studies (or higher) from the University of Strathclyde, or a Family History Skills & Strategy (Advanced) Distance Learning Certificate from Pharos / the Society of Genealogists.
- applying in the traditional way.
- moving from Associate to Member status.

A) Holding the Diploma in Genealogy:

- demonstrate ability to apply knowledge, convey findings clearly and act professionally in communicating with clients, by submitting one report commissioned by a client (including use of pre-1837 sources), with associated correspondence and at least one drop-line pedigree.

B) Holding a Higher Certificate or Post-Graduate Certificate or Advanced

---

[101] The reason for a holder of the Diploma in Genealogy not being required to submit a research assignment, as other applicants must, is that in obtaining the diploma they already will have successfully completed a research assignment set by the Institute, and an AGRA Member acts as External Moderator on this diploma examination.

Distance Learning Certificate:

- demonstrate ability to apply knowledge, convey findings clearly and act professionally in communicating with clients, by submitting <u>one</u> report commissioned by a client (including use of pre-1837 sources), with associated correspondence and at least one drop-line pedigree.

- undertake a research assignment set by the Board of Assessors, to involve a maximum of 20 hours, inclusive of report preparation.

C) Applying the traditional way:

- demonstrate the scope of knowledge using a wide range of original sources (not just transcripts) and techniques in submitting <u>three</u> examples of reports commissioned by clients (including use of pre-1837 sources, probate documents and parish registers / bishop's transcripts), with associated correspondence and at least one drop-line pedigree.

- undertake a research assignment set by the Board of Assessors, to involve a maximum of 20 hours, inclusive of report preparation.

D) Moving from Associate to Member status:

- complete the applicable requirements from A, B or C, above.

- provide evidence of CPD by submitting a CPD log.

Assessment Process

Membership applications are initially assessed by the Board of Assessors. The board comprises of AGRA Members with extensive experience. It may consult external experts in cases where applicants demonstrate knowledge of a subject unfamiliar to board members. The applicant is informed of the date and location of their interview and the starting point for the research assignment (if applicable). In the interview the applicant is given a sample of eighteenth or early nineteenth century handwriting that they will encounter in the course of research. They will be required to transcribe, understand and comment on the document's genealogical content. The research assignment and submitted examples of research reports are also discussed. If the board approves the application the applicant will accept the Code of Practice and pay the annual membership subscription.

Duration of Credentials

Credentials are linked to membership of AGRA. Members are encouraged to participate in CPD. Membership is retained indefinitely, on payment of an annual fee, unless disqualification occurs under disciplinary rules, following a serious complaint being upheld by the complaints panel, or for not complying with requirements in AGRA's constitution.

Obtaining Associate status

To be eligible to apply for Associate status one must:

- be operating or intending to operate a genealogical research service using English or Welsh records, or working towards a membership application.
- have a sound understanding of basic genealogical sources and the use of original documents.
- be resident in the British Isles.

What is involved in applying for Associate status:

An applicant must:

- apply online through the AGRA website.
- submit an application fee.
- hold or be working towards a Higher Certificate in Genealogy (or higher) from the Institute of Heraldic and Genealogical Studies, or a Post-Graduate Certificate in Genealogical, Palaeographic and Heraldic Studies (or higher) from the University of Strathclyde, or a Family History Skills & Strategy (Advanced) Distance Learning Certificate from Pharos / the Society of Genealogists, or be working to increase knowledge of genealogical sources and practices through other courses or learning methods.
- submit a business development plan.
- present for interview with the Board of Assessors, to demonstrate basic skills, to compile a drop-line family tree and to demonstrate basic palaeographic skills: interviews are held twice yearly.

Assessment Process

Applications for Associate status are initially assessed by the Board of Assessors. The applicant is informed of the date and location of their interview. If the Board approves the application the applicant will accept the Code of Practice and pay the annual Associate subscription.

Duration of Associate status

An Associate must participate in a structured programme of CPD, including AGRA study days and Network Group meetings and events. They may use the term AGRA Associate or Associate of AGRA but may not use the AGRA logo or imply that they are a Member. They may apply for membership after at least two years as an Associate and are expected to apply within five years of joining the Association.

ASSOCIATION OF SCOTTISH GENEALOGISTS AND RESEARCHERS IN ARCHIVES (ASGRA)

WEBSITE: www.asgra.co.uk

Overview

ASGRA was formed in 1981 as the Association of Scottish Genealogists and Record Agents. It changed its name to Association of Scottish Genealogists and Researchers in Archives in 2004 but retained the acronym ASGRA. In 2010 ASGRA entered a formal partnership with AGRA, which lasted to June 2017. In April 2016 ASGRA entered an alliance with AGI. The first Probationers were admitted in 2000. In 2015 the new category of Affiliate was brought in for those not practising as genealogists but whose association may be of mutual relevance and benefit. Fellowship was introduced in 2017 to recognise outstanding contribution by members.

ASGRA's Patron is the Lord Lyon King of Arms. The association has an Honorary President, elected for a four-year term, eligible for re-election at the annual general meeting. The President may be an external individual or come from within the membership, but is not part of ASGRA's governing Council. The Council includes a Chairman, Vice-Chairman, Honorary Secretary and Honorary Treasurer. Members and Associate Members of ASGRA of at least 12 months' standing are eligible for election as ordinary Council members. Ordinary Council members are elected for a two-year term and are eligible for re-election but may not remain ordinary Council members for more than four consecutive years, unless in exceptional circumstances. Council may co-opt additional members. To be eligible to become an officer, an ordinary Council member must have served at least 12 months on the Council. The officers are elected for a two-year term and are eligible for re-election annually, but may not hold the same office for more than four consecutive years, unless in exceptional circumstances. The annual general meeting is held in Edinburgh.

Geographical coverage

To obtain ASGRA credentials a genealogist or researcher in archives must be resident within the United Kingdom and involved in genealogical research in Scotland.

Code of Practice

Applicants for either Member or Probationer status must sign an agreement to abide by ASGRA's Code of Practice [www.asgra.co.uk/codeofpractice.php].

Complaints Investigation

A complaint is handled initially by the Chairman or a nominee, who will determine whether it should be brought before the Council. If the complaint goes before the Council the complainant is informed that the matter is being investigated. The Council will determine whether it is valid and, if so, whether it merits a written warning. Arrangements will be made for any outstanding work for the client to be completed, either by the original researcher or by another Member, within an agreed time limit. Following delivery of the report the complainant is contacted to enquire whether they are satisfied. The Council is empowered to order the researcher to return any pre-paid fee, or part thereof, to the client. If a researcher receives three written warnings and a further valid complaint is received, all within a three year period, the researcher will be removed from the ASGRA list.

Credential Categories

MEMBER: ASGRA accredits genealogists and researchers in archives, but there is only one credential category, that of Member, which may relate to either. A Member may be granted the status of Fellow (see below under 'Honorific Categories').

Honorific Categories

FELLOW: A Member may be granted the status of Fellow in recognition of service and contribution to ASGRA or the profession of genealogy.

Non-Credential Categories

AFFILIATE: An individual working in a position related to genealogy, but not practising as a genealogist, may be admitted as an Affiliate where affiliation is deemed by ASGRA's assessors to be of mutual relevance and benefit. There is a separate Code of Practice for Affiliates [www.asgra.co.uk/applicationbooklet.php].

ASSOCIATE MEMBER: A Member who takes on full-time employment outside the terms defined for a genealogist or researcher in archives may retain membership by becoming an Associate Member. This status is available either on a temporary or permanent basis at the discretion of the Council.

PROBATIONER: A genealogist or researcher in archives who may not have the necessary experience to apply for full membership of ASGRA has the option to apply to become a Probationer. There are two routes to Probationer status for genealogists. By the first route the applicant must submit two examples of reports commissioned by clients, obtain the clients' permission to submit the reports, and provide a brief note of the clients' original requests. One of these examples must be a direct male line genealogical study back to the late eighteenth century using standard sources: the other must be a study using other primary sources. The second route is for an applicant holding a post-graduate certificate / diploma from the University of Strathclyde or the University of Dundee. The requirement for supporting material depends on the level of the award and the date it was awarded. Applicants for Probationer status as (non-genealogical) researchers in archives should contact ASGRA for details of requirements. All applicants for this status must submit transcripts of two short examples from suitable manuscripts, chosen by ASGRA. All applicants must make a statement of intent to operate a genealogical or historical research business. A Probationer, if they wish, may be mentored by as ASGRA Member. They may not use the post-nominal initials ASGRA, or the ASGRA logo. A Probationer must participate in CPD. The period of probation is a maximum of two years before applying for full membership. If an application is not made within the required time the Probationer will be invited to re-apply. To become a Member a Probationer goes through the same process as any other applicant.

Post-Nominal Initials

ASGRA (denotes membership of the Association of Scottish Genealogists and Researchers in Archives)

FSGRA (denotes Fellow of the Association of Scottish Genealogists and Researchers in Archives)

Obtaining a Credential

MEMBER

To be eligible to apply for membership one must:

- be an experienced or suitably-qualified genealogist or researcher in archives.
- be resident in the United Kingdom.
- be currently practising in Scotland.
- be a self-employed genealogist or researcher in archives.
- not be in full-time employment outside that of (self-employed) genealogist or researcher in archives.

What is involved in applying for Credentials

An applicant must:

- submit a written statement of relevant experience (e.g. work undertaken on genealogy, local history or social history).
- make a statement of their operation of a genealogical or historical research business.
- sign an agreement to abide by the ASGRA Code of Practice.
- submit an application fee.

Additional criteria depend on the applicant's circumstance, as follows:

- genealogist applying in the traditional way.
- holding a post-graduate diploma in Genealogical, Palaeographic and Heraldic Studies from the University of Strathclyde or in Family and Local History from the University of Dundee.
- researcher in archives.

A) Applying the traditional way:

- submit a copy of a report (30 pages maximum) commissioned by a client, being a direct male line genealogical study back to the late eighteenth century, using standard sources. It is essential that the applicant is familiar with researching in the ScotlandsPeople Centre in Edinburgh even if the online alternative was employed in the search. The applicant must obtain permission from the client to submit the report and provide a brief note of the client's original request.

- submit a study (30 pages maximum) using other primary sources (e.g. records held in the National Archives of Scotland, local archives or university archives, including Kirk Session or other church records, court records, sasines, wills or valuation rolls).

- submit a study of the applicant's choice (30 pages maximum) which may involve an area of special interest.

- submit transcripts of two short examples from suitable manuscripts, chosen by ASGRA.

B) Holding a post-graduate diploma:

- submit a copy of the certificate or diploma and indicate any syllabus options.

- submit a sample report (which may be a course report).

- supply supporting material (usually requested by the Panel of Assessors) such as examples of work commissioned by clients or work completed for the genealogical studies course.

- submit transcripts of two short examples from suitable manuscripts, chosen by ASGRA.

- (additionally for those awarded the diploma before 2013) submit a sample recent report commissioned by a client.

C) Researcher in Archives:

- contact ASGRA for details of requirements.

- submit transcripts of two short examples from suitable manuscripts, chosen by ASGRA.

Assessment Process

Membership applications are assessed by the Panel of Assessors, comprising of three ASGRA Members. A standardised marking system is used. The system is overseen by an external assessment moderator. There are no bands, a successful applicant being awarded a 'pass'. Unsuccessful applicants receive a full assessment report. They may make a maximum of two further applications within two years. Successful applicants must be approved by the Council.

Duration of Credentials

Credentials are linked to membership of ASGRA. Members are encouraged to participate in CPD. Membership is retained indefinitely, on payment of an annual fee. The name of any Member, Associate, Probationer or Affiliate may be removed from ASGRA's list by resolution of the Members and Associates in general meeting, on the recommendation of the Council.

AUSTRALASIAN ASSOCIATION OF GENEALOGISTS AND RECORD AGENTS (AAGRA)

> WEBSITE: www.aagra.asn.au

Overview

AAGRA was formed in April 1977 and it was styled on the model of AGRA. Initially membership was by invitation, with a formal application process developing soon afterwards. Membership remains open to both genealogists and record agents. In November 2015 AAGRA introduced the new categories of Associate Member and Fellow.

AAGRA is governed by a Committee, comprising of officers (President, Vice-President, Honorary Secretary, Honorary Treasurer) and regional representatives, elected at each annual general meeting.

Geographical coverage

To obtain AAGRA credentials a genealogist or record agent must be practising within Australia or New Zealand.

Code of Ethics

Applicants for either membership must sign an undertaking to abide by AAGRA's Rules and Code of Ethics [www.aagra.asn.au/code-of-ethics].

Complaints Investigation

A client is advised to communicate dissatisfaction initially to the Member concerned. If the matter cannot be resolved it should be referred to the Secretary of AAGRA, after which it will be examined by the Committee.

Credential Categories

MEMBER (MAAGRA): Applicants for membership may apply in the category of **Genealogist** or **Record Agent** or both. As defined by AAGRA, a Genealogist 'compiles family histories and genealogies for clients and is often responsible for the publication of the finished product', while a Record Agent 'specialises in the researching of records and sources'. There are common requirements for both categories, with additional expectations for the Genealogist. A Record Agent may gain membership and later apply to be recognised additionally as a Genealogist. All accredited Members have equal rights within the association.

Honorifics Categories

FELLOW: A Member may be granted the status of Fellow in recognition of exceptional service to AAGRA or a particularly outstanding contribution to the study of Australasian genealogy.

Non-Credential Categories

ASSOCIATE MEMBER: A genealogist relatively new to professional research may apply for AAGRA Associate membership. They are not required to prove professional competence. It is expected that an Associate Member will progress to membership as a Record Agent or Genealogist within two years, having proved evidence of research and business competency.

Post-Nominal Initials or Terms

MAAGRA (denotes Member of the Australasian Association of Genealogists and Record Agents)

Obtaining a Credential

MEMBER

To be eligible to apply for membership one must:

- be actively engaged in the practice of genealogy or record searching.
- be currently practising in Australia or New Zealand.

What is involved in applying for Credentials

There is no application fee. An applicant must:

- complete and post the AAGRA Membership Application form [linked from this page: www.aagra.asn.au/membership] to The Secretary (address on the form).

Additional criteria depend on whether the application is as a Record Agent or as a Genealogist. It is possible to apply for both categories together:

A) Applying as a Record Agent, an applicant must:

- demonstrate ability in business skills, including business registrations.
- demonstrate ability in English expression, including any formal training.
- demonstrate ability in correct citation, including examples of work.
- demonstrate a thorough understanding of sources.

- demonstrate training / experience in handling original documents and manuscripts.

- submit research files for two clients for evaluation, including copies of correspondence with the client and copies of the research; permission should be sought from the clients and if privacy is requested the clients' names may be blocked out.

B) Applying as a Genealogist, an applicant must:

- fulfil all the same requirements as a Record Agent, above.

- demonstrate appropriate use of sources to provide basis for analytical research.

- demonstrate correct analysis of information and ability to document research rationale.

- demonstrate ability in a lateral range of sources, including summary of experiences to date.

- demonstrate ability with accepted genealogical charting methods, including computer skills.

- demonstrate ability in manuscript preparation, including lists of publications.

- submit at least one completed manuscript of a family history, and/ or copies of published family histories and/or genealogies; permission should be sought from the client.

Assessment Process

Membership applications are assessed by the Committee. No reason need be given for rejection of an application.

Duration of Credentials

Credentials are linked to membership of AAGRA. Membership is retained indefinitely, on payment of an annual fee, unless the Member resigns or is expelled.

BOARD FOR CERTIFICATION OF GENEALOGISTS (BCG)

WEBSITE: www.bcgcertification.org

Overview

BCG was formed in 1964 as the Board of Genealogical Certification, which soon became the Board for Certification of Genealogists. It is a certifying body rather than a membership organisation. Those certified are often referred to as associates. Originally BCG had two credential categories, Certified Genealogist [CG] and Certified Genealogical Record Searcher [CGRS]. Four new credential categories were introduced: Certified Genealogical Lecturer, Certified Genealogical Instructor, Certified American Lineage Specialist and Certified American Indian Lineage Specialist. The lineage specialist categories were later merged. Later still the lineage specialist certification joined the other two research categories in what is now the Certified Genealogist credential. The Certified Genealogical Instructor credential was also discontinued, leaving only two certification categories. Those accredited by BCG often are referred to in the USA as 'Board-certified'. BCG now recognises two categories of formerly certified associates by courtesy, with Emeritus Associate or Retired Associate status. BCG published *The BCG Genealogical Standards Manual* in 2000 and *Genealogy Standards* in 2014, while *The BCG Application Guide* may be accessed on its website.

BCG is governed by the Board of Trustees with fifteen members, all of whom are certified associates. Trustees are elected for a three-year term and they may be re-elected for a similar term after an interval from the board of two years. At each annual general meeting five trustees are elected. Since 2000 the election is by currently certified associates. The trustees appoint from among their number a President, Vice-President, Treasurer and Secretary, and one or more trustees, to serve on an Executive Committee. The day-to-day running of BCG is the responsibility of the Executive Committee, comprising the above and a Past-President. BCG also has a professional Executive Director. The annual general meeting is held in Washington, D.C.

Geographical coverage

There is no stated geographical limitation in relation to obtaining BCG certification. However, applications are adjudged in the English language. In the preliminary application form the option is given to state a language, in addition to English, that is involved in the genealogist's work. Part of the application process involves the interpretation of a document. *The BCG Application Guide* states: 'If your preliminary application stated an intention to work in a language other than English, the BCG-supplied document will likely be in that language. Your transcription must be in that language as well. *Include also a translation into standard English* and continue in English with the rest of the requirements'.[102] The vast majority of BCG-certified associates reside in the USA. As of January 2017 there were 225 certified persons listed on the BCG website, with 217 of them resident in the USA. A further eight certified persons were resident in Canada, France, the Netherlands and the United Kingdom.[103]

Code of Ethics

All those certified by BCG must sign and abide by the Genealogist's Code, which is the organisation's Code of Ethics [https://bcgcertification.org/ethics-standards/code].

Complaints Investigation

A complaint against a certified person must be made in writing to the President of BCG, accompanied by supporting evidence. Initially the President will try to resolve the dispute through mediation and agreement. Certified persons may also be subject to disciplinary action due to violation of the Genealogist's Code regardless of how this may come to the attention of the President. In both cases the process is confidential unless public sanctions are imposed. Unresolved disputes or disciplinary matters are brought before the Executive Committee, which may delegate the investigation to a member of the Board of Trustees. Once the Executive Committee is apprised of the situation the certified person is given the right to reply in writing within thirty days. After that a decision is made, with a two-thirds majority vote of the Executive Committee necessary. A range of actions may be taken, from dismissing the allegation as unfounded, to censure, to demanding the refunding of fees, to suspension or termination of certification. Public sanctions are taken only when compliance with lesser sanctions fails. The certified person may appeal the decision to the Board of Trustees within thirty days of receipt of the Executive Committee's decision. The Board's decision, by two-thirds majority, is final. The decision is included in the certified person's

---

[102] 'Requirements: CG Applications', sub-section 3-A, *The BCG Application Guide* (rev. 2017), 3-4, https://bcgcertification.org/wp-content/uploads/2017/10/BCG-Application-Guide-2017.pdf, accessed 18 July 2018.

[103] BCG, 'Directory', www.bcgcertification.org/associates/index.php, accessed 5 Jan. 2017 [page no longer active].

permanent file. A person who loses certification in this process may submit as a new applicant for certification only after a period of five years.

Credential categories

BCG now certifies genealogists only. There are two credential categories, those of Certified Genealogist and Certified Genealogical Lecturer.

CERTIFIED GENEALOGIST [CG]: This is the research category, in which the majority of associates are certified.

CERTIFIED GENEALOGICAL LECTURER [CGL]: To be eligible for this category one must already have certification in the research category [CG].

Honorific Categories

EMERITUS ASSOCIATE: At the discretion of the Board of Trustees, a retired, or semi-retired, certified associate who has had long connection with BCG may be granted the status of BCG Emeritus Associate.

RETIRED ASSOCIATE: This status is offered to those who have retired having been certified for more than twenty years.

Post-Nominal Initials or Terms

CG (denotes Certified Genealogist)

CGL (denotes Certified Genealogical Lecturer)

Obtaining a Credential

A) CERTIFIED GENEALOGIST [CG]:

There are no stated eligibility requirements and no specific educational requirements.

What is involved in applying for Credentials

An applicant must initially:

- complete a Preliminary Application Form stating the geographical area, time period or specialty subject (and, if applicable, any language other than English) in which they normally work, allowing BCG to select a suitable document to supply for the five 'treatments' in the final application portfolio (see below).
- submit a preliminary application fee.

- Having received an application package, and referring to BCG's publication *Genealogy Standards* for guidance, an applicant must (within one year from the date of the preliminary application):
- submit a Category Application Form.
- submit the final application portfolio (see below).
- submit a final application fee.

The final application portfolio will consist of:

- a signed, dated copy of BCG's Code of Ethics and Conduct, otherwise called the 'Genealogist's Code'.
- a list of activities relating to genealogy that helped the applicant prepare for the submission, indicating how they helped develop standards, knowledge and skills.
- five 'treatments' of the BCG-supplied document (selected as typical of records that may be encounter in research, based on the geographical area, time period, specialty subject or language outlined in the applicant's Preliminary Application Form), as follows.
- a) a transcription of the document; if the Preliminary Application Form mentioned a language other than English the document will likely be in that language and it must be transcribed in that language as well as being translated into standard English (the remaining four 'treatments' should be done in English only).
  b) an abstract of the document.
  c) a statement identifying a single research question based on the document.
  d) an analysis of the data in the document relating to the research question.
  e) a research plan describing initial steps towards resolving the research question.
- five 'treatments' (as with the BCG-supplied document, above) of a document of the applicant's choice.
- a report prepared for a (not necessarily fee-paying) commissioning client, exactly as it was sent to the client, along with copies of all document images that accompanied the original report, the client's authorisation for the search, and the client's written permission for use of the report in the portfolio.

- a case study drawn from the applicant's research demonstrating application of the 'Genealogical Proof Standard' (described in *Genealogy Standards*), and resolving a problem 'of *relationship* or *identity* that cannot be resolved from uncontested direct evidence'.

- a narrative genealogy, narrative lineage, or narrative pedigree, documenting and explaining 'linkages among individuals through three ancestral generations – ascending or descending'.

Assessment process

Portfolios are reviewed by three of BCG's approximately 45 judges, all of whom are certified associates. The judges conduct their evaluation without reference to one another, and their identities are not revealed, while their comments are conveyed to the applicant. If the judges' decision is not unanimous the portfolio is passed to another judge for further assessment. The fourth judge reviews the portfolio and the other judges' evaluations before making a decision on the application. An unsuccessful applicant may appeal the decision to the Board of Trustees. A two-thirds majority vote is needed to overturn the judges' decision.

B) CERTIFIED GENEALOGICAL LECTURER [CGL]:

To be eligible to apply for certification in this category one must already be certified in the research category [CG].

What is involved in applying for the lecturing Credential

Having already achieved certification in the research category [CG], an applicant must:

- submit a Category Application Form.
- submit the application portfolio (see below).
- submit an application fee.
- The application portfolio will consist of:
- a background résumé summarising lecturing activities, and listing genealogical topics competent to present.
- digital recordings of two genealogical lectures presented
- a copy of the script, outline or speaking notes used.
- a copy of the accompanying handout.

- copies of accompanying visual aids.

- a list of materials the applicant recommends for further study on the topic (if not included in the accompanying handout).

Assessment process

Portfolios for the lecturing category are reviewed in the same way as those for the research category [CG] (see above).

Duration of Credentials

Certification by BCG is not permanent. CGs must apply every five years for renewal of their credentials. They must submit their renewal application in advance of the expiration of their current certification. Lecturing credentials for CGLs expire at the same time as their research credentials do. They may apply simultaneously for both research and lecturing category renewals.

BUREAU QUÉBÉCOIS D'ATTESTATION
DE COMPÉTENCE EN GÉNÉALOGIE (BQACG)

WEBSITE: http://federationgenealogie.qc.ca/bureau-attestation

Overview

BQACG was established by the *Fédération québécoise des sociétés de généalogie* (FQSG) in 1991. It provides credentials for genealogists throughout Quebec but to be eligible for accreditation an applicant must be a member of a genealogical society affiliated to the FQSG.

The Bureau is run by three people, appointed by the administrative council of the FQSG, one of whom must be an accredited genealogist. The Bureau's three members are the President, the Vice-President and the Secretary. It appoints the judges who assess applications for credentials. Prior to 2010 the Bureau consisted of five members.

Geographical coverage

To obtain BQACG credentials a genealogist must be a member of a genealogical society affiliated to the *Fédération québécoise des sociétés de généalogie*, but this does not mean that they must be resident in Quebec.

Code of Ethics (*Code d'éthique*)

Those applying for accreditation must agree to abide by the *Code d'éthique du généalogiste* of the FQSG [http://federationgenealogie.qc.ca/guide-ressources/code-d-ethique-du-genealogiste].

Complaints Investigation

Any violation of the *Code d'éthique* brought to the attention of the FQSG may be subject to a penalty, but only after an investigation in which the accredited genealogist concerned has had a right to be heard on the allegation.

Credential categories

BQACG has three levels of credentials. The initial level is that of *Généalogiste de filiation agréé* / Certified Lineage Genealogist. It is necessary to hold the credential of this level to progress to *Généalogiste recherchiste agréé* / Certified Genealogical Researcher. Similarly, it is necessary to hold the second credential to progress to the third, *Maître généalogiste agréé* / Certified Master Genealogist. Theoretically, a combined application for all three levels could be made at the same time.

Honorific Categories

Généalogiste émérite: This designation is not directly linked to the awards by BQACG. It was established by the FQSG in 1984 to recognise the contribution made by individuals to the development of genealogy. Those awarded the status in 1984 were mainly founding members of genealogical societies or those known for their publications. It was not until 2008 that other individuals were awarded the designation. These were recognised for work on computerised research tools or for administration within the FQSG or an affiliated society. No further awards were made after 2008 but significant contributions to genealogy have since been recognised with the FQSG *Médaille d'honneur*. In April 2013 the designation *Généalogiste émérite* was withdrawn but it may be revived to highlight an exceptional contribution. Those awarded it in 1984 and 2008 continue to be recognised.

Post-Nominal Initials or Terms

GFA (*Généalogiste de filiation agréé* / Certified Lineage Genealogist)

GRA (*Généalogiste recherchiste agréé* / Certified Genealogical Researcher)

MGA (*Maître généalogiste agréé* / Certified Master Genealogist)

Obtaining a Credential

ALL CATEGORIES

- To be eligible to apply for a credential one must:
- be a member of one of the more than seventy genealogical societies affiliated to the FQSG.
- agree to abide by the *Code d'éthique* of the FQSG.

What is involved in applying for credentials

AN APPLICANT MUST

- submit an administrative file containing a completed and signed registration form, a copy of the applicant's up-to-date membership card of a society affiliated to the FQSG, an agreement to abide by the *Code d'éthique* of the FQSG, and an application fee.
- submit a portfolio containing the applicant's submission for credentials

(content depends on the credential sought, see below).

- pass a written examination, after which the portfolio is assessed; the examinations take place in Quebec and Montreal, or alternatively on the premises of the applicant's society affiliated to the FQSG.

Additional requirements depend on the credential sought, as follows:

A) *Généalogiste de filiation agréé* / Certified Lineage Genealogist

IN THE PORTFOLIO

- construct an ancestral fan-chart comprising ten generations with (from official documents) forenames and surnames of husband and wife, and date and place of marriage or date of marriage contract and name of notary; use a numbering system such as Stradonitz and in an appendix give additional information.

- present copies of marriage records or marriage contracts, confirming an ancestral line of at least eight generations, with each document referenced.

- write grammatically in the chosen language (French or English).

IN THE EXAMINATION

- identify research sources, showing knowledge of their characteristics, content and limitations.

- use the various research sources provided in the examination to find genealogical information.

B) *Généalogiste recherchiste agréé* / Certified Genealogical Researcher

- must have obtained the *Généalogiste de filiation agréé* / Certified Lineage Genealogist credential or may submit a combined application for both credentials.

IN THE PORTFOLIO

- present the results of a search, giving the information contained in baptismal, marriage and burial records and of other supporting documents, on four lines from paternal or maternal grandparents, covering at least seven generations including the grandparents.

- outline a work plan for a research project, including objectives, detailed plan of action and sources consulted or to be consulted.

- write a genealogical text suitable for publication, involving advanced research, and including references, a bibliography, sources for illustrations and relevant permissions.

- develop an information classification model, organising the information so that it is easy to locate, and including supporting information.

- write grammatically in the chosen language (French or English).

IN THE EXAMINATION

- identify research sources (other than those specified for the *Généalogiste de filiation agréé* / Certified Lineage Genealogist, above) and a wide range of advanced research sources, showing knowledge of their characteristics, content and limitations.

- extract the pertinent information from a manuscript provided in the examination.

- solve complex problems presented in the examination, explaining the approach taken.

C) *Maître généalogiste agréé* / Certified Master Genealogist

- must have obtained the *Généalogiste de filiation agréé* / Certified Lineage Genealogist and the *Généalogiste recherchiste agréé* / Certified Genealogical Researcher credentials or may submit a combined application for all three credentials; must have an interview with the judges.

IN THE PORTFOLIO

- design a plan for a course, provide a description, define the objectives, outline presentations and schedule and design a bibliography.

- supply an outline of a presentation, with the date and place it was given (if applicable).

- supply details of writing and publishing (individually or in collaboration) genealogical works and research tools (with the exception of works merely requiring compilation), describe the work of the author with an editor, demonstrate the relevance of writing on the subject or of developing the research tool, and indicate the method of circulation used.

- write grammatically in the chosen language (French or English).

IN THE EXAMINATION

- transcribe, word-for-word, manuscripts, provided in the examination, resolving problems with a degree of difficulty and using the rules of palaeography, adding the full term in parentheses for abbreviations, and indicating the meaning of Old French words no longer in use.

Assessment process

Applications for credentials are treated as confidential and the identity of the acting judges is not revealed. The judges are chosen by the Bureau from among those accredited at the level for which the applicant is applying, or at a higher level, or from specialists of recognised competence in a field relevant to the case to be assessed. Each judge draws up a report and passes it to the President. The judges' decision is by a majority. The President condenses the judges' reports into one and sends it to the applicant. If the application is successful the applicant is sent a certificate of competence and an announcement is made at the next annual general meeting. If the application is unsuccessful the applicant is notified in writing and they are entitled to reapply whenever they wish.

Duration of Credentials

Credentials are retained indefinitely, regardless of whether the genealogist remains a member of the affiliated society through which they applied for accreditation. The only circumstance in which credentials may be lost is in the case of a proven breach of the *Code d'éthique*.

GENEALOGICAL INSTITUTE OF THE MARITIMES (GIM)

WEBSITE: http://nsgna.ednet.ns.ca/gim

Overview

In 1983 the Genealogical Institute of the Maritimes (GIM) was established for certification and registration of genealogical researchers in New Brunswick, Nova Scotia and Prince Edward Island. Newfoundland was added to its area in 1986. From its foundation GIM provided credentials for genealogical record searchers as well as genealogists. Those admitted to accreditation become members of GIM.

Geographical coverage

To obtain GIM credentials a genealogist or record searcher must be practising within Canada and using the genealogical sources of one of the four provinces of Atlantic Canada.

Code of Ethics

Those admitted to membership must sign an undertaking to abide by GIM's Code of Ethics.

Complaints Investigation

Complaints come to the President through the Registrar. The President either meets or communicates with the Member identified in the complaint, asks for their reaction and for how they plan to deal with it. If the Member is unable to deal with the complaint to the satisfaction of the client, the matter goes to the Board of GIM to decide on whether the complaint is justified.

Credential Categories

GIM has two credential categories.

Genealogical Record Searcher [Canada].

Certified Genealogist [Canada].

Those admitted to either become Members of GIM.

Honorifics Categories

None

Non-Credential Categories

None

Post-Nominal Initials or Terms

GRS(C) (denoted Genealogical Record Searcher [Canada])

CG(C) (denotes Certified Genealogist [Canada])

Obtaining a Credential

The entire application process may be completed in either English or French. The initial stage for either of the two membership categories is completion of the preliminary application form, with the applicant assigning points to themselves for the areas of Education, Experience and Publication. This indicates to the applicant and to the GIM assessors whether they are eligible to proceed. At least 7 points are needed for Genealogical Record Searcher category and at least 14 for Certified Genealogist, with at least two points coming from each of the three areas.

The areas are as follows:

- Education (maximum 8 points): points awarded for four levels of general education from a university degree down to high school attendance without a diploma; additional points (maximum 4 of the 8 points) available for having taught or attended a genealogical course.
- Experience (maximum 14 points): a point awarded for each year of work in genealogical records (maximum 10) and up to 4 points available for participation in genealogical organisations.
- Publication (maximum 6 points): points awarded for books, articles or unpublished collections available to the public, relating to genealogy, biography, demography or history.

In addition, the applicant must:

- append a report briefly explaining the points claimed in each area.
- provide the names and contact details of three people familiar with their qualifications, stating these persons' positions in genealogical organisation or archival institution.
- attest to the information in the form being an accurate representation of eligibility.

- pay a preliminary application fee.
- If the application is successful, the applicant must:
- submit a formal application.
- pay a certification fee.

Additional criteria depend on which of the two categories of membership is involved:

A) Applying as a Genealogical Record Searcher, an applicant must:
- prepare a report on a research problem of their choice demonstrating their ability to locate genealogical sources, research, cite or document sources, and provide copies or abstracts of documents.
- (if the report is satisfactory) sit a written examination.
- attend an interview where the report and examination are discussed.

B) Applying as a Certified Genealogist, an applicant must:
- prepare a work sample (20 pages maximum) demonstrating their ability to research, analyse, organise, record and footnote a family history.
- (if the work sample is satisfactory) sit a written examination.
- attend an interview where the work sample and examination are discussed.

Assessment Process

Assessments and examinations are conducted by a Board of Examiners of GIM, consisting of two Certified Genealogists from each of the four Atlantic provinces.

Following acceptance of the preliminary application form, the report or work sample is submitted. This is assigned to three members of the Examining Board, who grade it and comment on its strengths and weaknesses. Successful candidates are invited to sit the written examination. Each assessment and examination is marked independently by the three board members and the applicant receives the average of the marks. Subsequently the interview is held. At this point the final decision is made.

Duration of Credentials

Credentials are retained indefinitely.

INTERNATIONAL COMMISSION FOR THE ACCREDITATION OF PROFESSIONAL GENEALOGISTS (ICAPGen)

WEBSITE: www.icapgen.org

Overview

The Accredited Genealogist credential was established in 1964 on the initiative of the Genealogical Society of Utah. Those receiving the credential were accredited rather than being members of an organisation. In 1999 the GSU decided to end its involvement with the credential. It asked the Utah Genealogical Association to help create an organisation to continue the work. In February 2000 the UGA appointed an Accreditation Committee which developed into the International Commission for the Accreditation of Professional Genealogists (ICAPGen). ICAPGen is an accrediting body rather than a membership organisation. Those receiving its credential are often referred to as AG professionals. In 2002 ICAPGen introduced Emeritus status for retiring AG professionals 'in good standing'. It published *Becoming an Excellent Genealogist: Essays on Professional Research Skills*, in 2012 and its *Guide to Applying for an Accredited Genealogist® Credential* may be assessed on its website.

ICAPGen is governed by a Board of Commissioners with twelve members, all of whom are AG professionals. Six members are elected for a three-year term and they may remain without re-election for a further three years. Elections are not necessarily held each year, occurring only when vacancies arise. Five members are appointed for a one-year term but their term may be extended. These members are appointed because of their qualifications in such areas as testing or education, or because of their position in a major archives or library. The Board's main officers are the President, Vice-President, Past President, Executive Secretary and Treasurer. The Board meets every two months in Salt Lake City.

Geographical coverage

There is no stated geographical limitation regarding residency in relation to obtaining ICAPGen credentials. Currently, the commission offers credentials for research in eight regions of the USA and on 24 countries or regions in rest of the world. These include Canada, Mexico, the British Isles, Scandinavia (including Finland) and most countries in the west and centre of Continental Europe, with

Germany divided into three regions.[104] Changes to these regions come into effect in the first quarter of 2019. There will then be nine regions in the USA, some with basic language requirements in French, German, Spanish or Swedish. There will be four (as opposed to the current two) regions in Canada. ICAPGen is currently developing new tests. These are an African-American Specialty (to be added to certain US regions) and regional tests for Brazil, Hungary, Portugal, Russia and South Africa.[105] A different examination is given for each geographical region.[106] The majority of AG professionals reside in Utah. As of January 2017 there were 151 AGs listed on the ICAPGen website, with 114 of them resident in Utah. All but two of the remaining 37 were resident in other parts of the USA.[107]

Code of Ethics

All those accredited by ICAPGen must sign and abide by the organisation's Code of Ethics [www.icapgen.org/professional-ethics/code-of-ethics].

Complaints Investigation

When a complaint about an accredited person is made to ICAPGen it is registered and pertinent facts are obtained from the complainant. An inquiry is opened, the accredited person is informed of the nature of the complaint and they respond. ICAPGen acts as a mediator between the two parties. If action is required by either party, a reasonable amount of time is allowed. An unresolved action or a fairly serious initial violation will usually result in a formal warning. A more serious case may involve the convening of a review board to consider the matter. If the complaint is upheld, disciplinary action may be taken, up to temporary suspension or revocation of accreditation.

Credential categories

ACCREDITED GENEALOGIST [AG]: ICAPGen accredits genealogists only. There is one credential category, that of Accredited Genealogist. To gain the credential an applicant must first pass the non-credential categories of Level 1 and Level 2.

---

[104] ICAPGen, 'Testing Regions', www.icapgen.org/testing-regions, accessed 18 July 2018.

[105] ICAPGen, 'Important Testing Announcements', posted 6 June 2018, https://icapgen.blog/2018/06/06/important-testing-announcements, accessed 18 July 2018.

[106] ICAPGen, 'Guide to Applying for an Accredited Genealogist Credential', https://www.icapgen.org//wp-content/uploads/2017/12/Guide-to-Applying-for-an-AG-Credential.pdf, 4, accessed 18 July 2018.

[107] ICAPGen, 'Find an AG Professional > By Residence', www.icapgen.org/find-an-ag-professional/by-residence, accessed 5 Jan. 2017.

Honorific Categories

EMERITUS AG PROFESSIONAL: Current AGs who decide to retire from professional research are offered the honorary status of Emeritus AG professional or Emeritus Accredited Genealogist during retirement. They may continue to lecture, write or research on a voluntary basis.

Non-Credential Categories

LEVEL 1: To progress to the credential category of Accredited Genealogist an applicant must advance through two lower levels of testing. To advance past Level 1 the applicant must have attained a score of at least 90% in its main test.

LEVEL 2: To advance to Level 3 the applicant must have attained a score of at least 90% in sections 1-4 of the written examination (sections 5-6 are part of the Level 3 test). Success at Level 3 qualifies the applicant for the credential of Accredited Genealogist.

Post-Nominal Initials or Terms

AG (denotes Accredited Genealogist)

Emeritus AG (denotes Emeritus Accredited Genealogist)

Obtaining a Credential

ACCREDITED GENEALOGIST [AG]

To be eligible to apply for credentials one must advance through the two preliminary levels of testing before testing at Level 3. The written examination part of the testing is divided into six sections, with the first four at Level 2 and the last two at Level 3. The *Guide to Applying for an Accredited Genealogist® Credential* should be of assistance in understanding the process. There is no requirement for formal training. An applicant may have acquired knowledge through a formal course, or through attending conferences or short courses, or through self-directed education. To be eligible to apply for Level 1 one must:

- have a minimum of 1,000 hours of combined genealogical research and genealogical education, with more than 500 of those hours devoted to the records of the chosen geographical accreditation region.

- have a minimum of 80 of those hours in five or more administrative divisions of the chosen international accreditation region, or a minimum of 80 of those hours in each state of the chosen US accreditation region.
- have, in addition to the minimum 80 hours outlined above, a minimum of 80 hours using nationwide genealogical records for the chosen geographical accreditation region.
- An applicant with an existing credential (e.g., an AG or a Certified Genealogist) may apply with half the required 1,000 experience hours.

What is involved in applying for Level 1

An applicant must:

- complete a questionnaire relating to the eligibility requirements above.
- submit a contact information form.
- submit an application fee.
- submit a report (25-40 pages in length) on a four-generation research project representing four connecting generations who lived within the same geographical region, accompanied by a pedigree chart, family group records, supporting documents and a research log. The most recent generation must have been born at least 80 years before the submission of the application.
- Successful completion of the questionnaire and achieving a mark of at least 90% on the four-generation research project will attain Level 1 status.

What is involved in applying for Level 2

An applicant must:

- within three years of successfully completing Level 1, apply for the written examination for Level 2.
- submit an application fee.
- sit the written examination, scheduled once a quarter, in Salt Lake City (or by special arrangement at another time or elsewhere); for the examination (lasting four hours, including breaks) the applicant is given use of one computer for research and another for testing; the examination is divided into four sections, testing (section 1) general knowledge of the history, geography, research methods and records of

the chosen accreditation region, (section 2) reading and transcribing handwriting in a document related to the relevant geographical area and time period (if the applicant is testing in a region with a language other than English they will be expected to translate a document of genealogical significance written in that language), (section 3) recognition of important types of documents and reference sources for the chosen accreditation region, and (section 4) knowledge of the content of online sources and electronic databases relating to the chosen accreditation region.

Achieving a mark of at least 90% on the written examination (sections 1-4) will attain Level 2 status.

What is involved in applying for Level 3 (Accreditation)

An applicant must:

- within three years of successfully completing Level 2, apply for the examination for Level 3.
- submit an application fee.
- sit the written examination, scheduled once a quarter, in Salt Lake City (or by special arrangement at another time or elsewhere); for the examination (lasting four hours, including breaks) the applicant is given use of one computer for research and another for testing; the examination is divided into two sections, testing (section 5) the ability to analyse a research problem and to plan appropriate research and (section 6) the ability within a period od three hours to conduct a search and write a report on it, also returning a research log, a pedigree chart, family group records and copies of documents.
- having achieved a mark of at least 90% on the written examination (sections 5-6), the applicant must present for a two-hour oral review (which may be conducted by video chat service for those who did not sit the examination in Salt Lake City) during which AGs from the chosen accreditation region will ask questions based on the applicant's tests and relating to the region.
- Successfully passing the oral review, having achieved all the other tests, will entitle the applicant to Accredited Genealogist status. At this point they must sign a Professional Ethics Agreement, which includes ICAPGen's Code of Ethics.

Assessment process

The three levels are coordinated by the testing committee.

Duration of Credentials

Accreditation by ICAPGen is not permanent. AGs must apply every five years for renewal of their credentials. They are reminded one year prior to the expiration date, and again six months and three months beforehand.

APPENDIX CI

Licensing in France

GÉNÉALOGISTES DE FRANCE

WEBSITE: http://genealogistes-france.org

Overview

Généalogistes de France was formed in 2004 as the *Union des Syndicats de Généalogistes Professionnels*. It is the representative and licensing organisation for most professional genealogists in France, both *généalogistes familiaux* (conducting traditional genealogical research) and *généalogistes successoraux* (conducting genealogical research related to probate or inheritance). For licensing, individual genealogists must be members of one of the six associations or chambers that subscribe to *Généalogistes de France* (see below). Of these, only SYGENE and CGP represent *généalogistes familiaux*. By far the greatest number of genealogists in France are *généalogistes successoraux*.

The six associations apparently have similar application criteria in terms of eligibility and similar vetting processes. While they do not appear to have any formal accreditation processes, they provide an assurance of the competence of their adherents. *Généalogistes de France* has a partnership with the *Conseil Supérieur du Notariat*, representing notaries throughout France. In December 2016, at the suggestion of *Généalogistes de France*, the national commission for consumer mediation appointed an ombudsman for the professional genealogy sector.

Code of Practice (*Charte déontologique des généalogistes professionnels*):

Those joining one of the associations and obtaining a professional card from *Généalogistes de France* must agree to abide by the *Charte déontologique des généalogistes professionnels* [http://genealogistes-france.org/qui-sommes-nous/presentation-de-lunion].

Constituent Syndicates

Chambre des Généalogistes Professionnels (CGP)
[https://www.cgpro.org/]

Chambre des Généalogistes Successoraux de France (CGSF)
[https://www.chambre-genealogistes.com/fr/]

Chambre Internationale des Généalogistes Professionnels (CIGP)
[http://cigp.weebly.com/]

Chambre Syndicale des Généalogistes de France (CSGF)

Compagnie Européenne des Généalogistes Successoraux (CEGS)
[http://www.cegs.eu/]

SYGENE, *l'alliance des généalogistes professionnels*
[http://www.sygene.fr/]

APPENDIX CII

Towards Accreditation for German-speaking Genealogists

VERBAND DEUTSCHSPRACHIGER BERUFSGENEALOGEN (ASSOCIATION OF GERMAN-SPEAKING PROFESSIONAL GENEALOGISTS)

WEBSITE: www.berufsgenealogie.net

Overview

Verband deutschsprachiger Berufsgenealogen was founded on 12 September 1992. It is an incorporated society, registered with the District Court of Charlottenburg. It does not claim to be an accrediting organisation, but its practices are quite close to those of most organisations providing credentials and it is working on an accreditation system.

The organisation is governed by a Board consisting of a chairperson and two deputy chairmen, elected each year at the annual general meeting, which usually takes place in September at the German genealogical conference.

Geographical Coverage

There is no residential requirement for membership, but proficiency in the German language is a prerequisite.

Code of Practice

Those admitted to membership must sign and abide by the organisation's Professional Rules of Conduct [www.berufsgenealogie.net/english/files/Professional-Rules-of-Conduct.pdf]. These cover research practices as well as conduct towards colleagues and clients.

Complaints Investigation

If a complaint is made against a member, the member is obliged to inform the organisation's arbitration board.

Obtaining Membership

To be eligible for membership the applicant must be earning at least part of their income from genealogical research. They must submit a sample research report. If this is considered to be of a sufficient standard the applicant is asked to attend an interview at which they are questioned on relevant topics, such as the ability to read old German script and knowledge of sources and archives in their specified region. Usually two of those conducting the interview specialise in that region.

APPENDIX CIII

Accrediting Bodies in Specialist Areas

COUNCIL FOR THE ADVANCEMENT
OF FORENSIC GENEALOGY (CAFG)

WEBSITE: www.forensicgenealogists.org

Overview

CAFG's definition of 'forensic genealogy' differs from that originally coined by Colleen Fitzpatrick in that it excludes the work conducted by traditional legal genealogists or heir searchers. CAFG was registered in May 2011 in the State of Texas. It was described as a 'business league with a professional membership' when it was announced on 19 July 2011. CAFG is governed by an elected Board of Directors with five members, four of whom occupy the offices of President, Vice-President, Secretary and Treasurer. It held its first 'Forensic Genealogy Institute' on 25-27 October 2012 in Dallas, Texas. This became an annual event, held earlier in the year, but it appears not to have taken place in 2018.

From its inception CAFG had a Mentor Program and then two levels of membership. In 2012 those enrolled in the Mentor Program became Associate Members and the other two levels became Junior Members and Advanced Members. In June 2014 the membership categories changed, with four instead of the former three. The categories became Levels I to IV, with Level I for new entrants and Level IV to be attained before being eligible to apply for the ForensicGenealogistCredentialed (FGC) accreditation. Early in 2018 the membership levels were renamed. Levels I, II, III and IV became Peer Mentor Program (the entry level), Associate, Junior and Senior. All four levels of membership have requirements beyond simply paying a fee and promising to abide by the Standards of Practice and Conduct. Having attained what is now Senior level a member is eligible to apply for the FGC accreditation.

In March 2015 CAFG awarded the first two FGC designations. In March 2018 it was announced that CAFG had awarded its first fellowship.

Geographical Coverage

There is no geographical coverage specified, but CAFG is based in the USA and it has Members in Canada.

Standards of Practice and Conduct

Those admitted to membership of CAFG must agree to abide by the organisation's Standards of Practice and Conduct [www.forensicgenealogists.org/standards].

Complaints Investigation

This is not outlined on CAFG's website.

Credential Categories

FORENSICGENEALOGISTCREDENTIALED: To attain this credential one must progress through four levels of membership of CAFG. Though FGC is the only 'credential' issued by CAFG, Associate, Junior and Senior Members are listed on CAFG's online Directory, so they are given here as a Credential Categories.

SENIOR MEMBER: Formerly known as Level IV, this is the highest level of membership.

JUNIOR MEMBER: This was known as Level III. To attain this level a Member must have progressed from Associate Member level.

ASSOCIATE MEMBER: This was known as Level II. It is the lowest level that merits listing on CAFG's online Directory.

Honorific Categories

FELLOW: A Member may be granted the status of Fellow in recognition of outstanding contributions to CAFG and 'forensic genealogy'.

Non-Credential Categories

PEER MENTOR PROGRAM: This is the entry level for membership of CAFG. As CAFG's online Directory does not list Members from this level, Peer Mentor Program is given here as a Non-Credential Category. As of June 2018, CAFG's website did not have updated information on the application process and membership level progression requirements. The 'Join' page was 'currently being updated'.[108] For that reason, the requirements stated here, as well as those below for the Associate, Junior and Senior Member levels, as those which pertained until early 2018 for the equivalent levels (I to IV).

To be eligible to apply one must have completed two of a list of approved courses 'or their equivalent approved by CAFG'. In addition to a variety of 'institutes', conferences and longer courses, the 'equivalents' include holding the AG or CG credential, having a degree in genealogy or being recognised by a court or government agency as an expert witness in genealogy. The following must be submitted:

- an application form.

- a signed copy of the CAFG Standards of Practice and Conduct.

- a résumé.

- a 'well-written, source-cited genealogical research report' completed within the past five years.

- a personal statement on why the applicant wants to be a forensic genealogist.

If accepted, the applicant must pay the membership fee.

Post-Nominal Initials or Terms

FGC (denotes ForensicGenealogistCredentialed)

Obtaining a Credential

ASSOCIATE MEMBER

- To attain this level one must:

- have attained all the requirements for Peer Mentor Program level (see above, Non-Credential Categories).

- have completed 100 hours of professional genealogical research.

- submit a 'well-written, source-cited genealogical research report or affidavit' completed within the past five years.

JUNIOR MEMBER

- To attain this level one must:

- have attained all the requirements for Associate Member level.

---

[108] CAFG, 'Join', www.forensicgenealogists.org/join, accessed 18 July 2018.

- have completed two years of substantial and continuous work as a professional genealogist.

- have completed 200 hours of forensic work within the past five years.

- submit a 'well-written, source-cited genealogical research report or affidavit' completed within the past five years.

SENIOR MEMBER

To attain this level one must:

- have attained all the requirements for Junior Member level.

- have completed three years of substantial and continuous work as a forensic genealogist.

- have completed 750 hours of forensic work within the past ten years.

- submit a 'well-written, source-cited genealogical research report or affidavit' completed within the past five years.

ForensicGenealogistCredentialed [FCG]

To attain this credential one must be a Senior Member of CAFG. The application process is in two parts. For Part I the applicant must:

- pay the application fee.

- submit a detailed résumé.

- submit a spreadsheet or list of at least 750 hours of substantial and continual work as a forensic genealogist within the past ten years.

- submit a Part I application form

If the Part I application is accepted, Part II may be started. For this the applicant must:

- pay the additional application fee.

- submit a forensic genealogy report, affidavit or article (a report previously submitted for membership advancement may be used as long as it is not modified).

- review an affidavit and answer questions on it.

- select a death certificate, obituary, will, deed or naturalisation paper supplied by CAFG and write on its criteria.

- answer (in a few sentences) a series of eleven questions, using any research sources in the process.

Assessment Process

Applications for each level of membership are assessed by a membership committee made up of existing Members. Applications for the FGC credential are assessed by two evaluators, with an overall of at least 80% to pass. If the evaluators require further information it may be necessary for the applicant to have an interview with a third evaluator.

Duration of Credentials

Members on all levels must complete fifteen hours of CPD classes and pay the annual membership fee to retain their status. The FGC credential is not permanent. Holders of the credential must apply every five years for renewal. The credential may be revoked for failure to pay the annual CAFG membership fee, for violation of the Standards of Practice and Conduct, or for illegal or unethical conduct

Glossary

ACCREDITING ORGANISATION

An organisation that evaluates the work of professional genealogists and provides them with credentials. It also facilitates resolution of any disputes that may arise between those it accredits and their clients. Some accrediting bodies operate as boards that issue credentials, while in other cases the credential is admission to membership of the organisation. Each one has its own system of evaluation. Information on the various accrediting bodies, and similar associations, is given in APPENDIXES C, C i, C ii and C iii.

CONTINUING PROFESSIONAL DEVELOPMENT (CPD)

Many accrediting bodies in genealogy encourage CPD among those holding their credentials. Continuing professional development is a way of keeping abreast of new sources, trends and practices through self-directed learning. AGI, AGRA and ASGRA organise CPD events for their members and expect them to pursue their own CPD through reading, attending lectures and exploring new sources. CPD is now mandatory for AGI Members and Affiliates, with quarterly CPD accounts to be submitted.

FORENSIC GENEALOGY

A term coined in 2005 by Colleen Fitzpatrick to describe the application of genealogical expertise to legal matters, otherwise referred to as legal or probate genealogy, or heir searching. The term forensic genealogist, as used by the Council for the Advancement of Forensic Genealogy, specifically excludes practitioners who conduct speculative research and seek a percentage of the inheritance of the heirs they identify.

GENERAL MEMBERSHIP ORGANISATION

An organisation or society for anyone interested in the subject, with no membership requirements beyond payment of an annual fee. The names of the larger or more significant or geographically important genealogical societies are given in APPENDIX B.

GENETIC GENEALOGY

The use of DNA testing to augment genealogical research through identifying common ancestral lines and estimating genealogical relationships between individuals.

HEIR SEARCHER

A term used (more so in the USA, it would appear) for a legal or probate genealogist. The term belies the range of research that may be carried out by such a practitioner. The Council for the Advancement of Forensic Genealogy applies the term only to those heir searchers who conduct speculative research and seek a percentage of the inheritance of the heirs they identify.

INSTITUTE

In the context of genealogy in the USA, an 'institute' is a short intensive course of lectures, run over a number of days. The first of these, the National Institute on Genealogical Research, was established in 1950 as a week-long event for experienced researchers. It has been held annually ever since, though now it is called Gen-Fed (Genealogical Institute on Federal Records). Today there are several similar courses in the USA styled as 'institutes'. Elsewhere the word retains its traditional meaning of an organisation (rather than a course) with a particular purpose, especially involving science, education or a particular profession. One of the world's accrediting organisations is the Genealogical Institute of the Maritimes. Also in Canada, the National Institute for Genealogical Studies is an online educational organisation, while the Institute of Heraldic and Genealogical Studies is a similar body based in England.

LEGAL / PROBATE GENEALOGY

The application of genealogical expertise to legal matters, including the identification of heirs to an estate and cases of adoption. In addition to genealogical expertise, a practitioner must acquire knowledge of the legal requirements of the various jurisdictions and skills in presenting information for or in court. Another term for a legal genealogist is 'heir searcher', though this does not accurately reflect the scope of the work involved. In the USA the term 'forensic genealogist' has come into use to describe the practice.

RECORD AGENT / RECORD SEARCHER

The term 'record agent' or 'record searcher' has slightly different meanings in different places. In one sphere the genealogist directs the research while the record agent conducts the searches; in another the genealogist compiles family histories / genealogies while, separately, the record agent specialises in searching records. Both AGRA and ASGRA changed their names to clarify the status of the non-genealogist members, the organisations becoming the Association of Genealogists and Researchers in Archives and the Association of Scottish Genealogists and Researchers in Archives. Today in these organisations there appears to be no real distinction between the categories 'genealogist' and 'researcher in archives'. The Board for Certification of Genealogists discontinued its Certified Genealogical Record Searcher category, merging it with Certified Genealogist. AAGRA retains the term 'record agent' in its title and the separate category of membership. GIM also retains separate categories.

STRADONITZ

A numbering system for recording direct ancestors, beginning with the subject as No. 1. The father is No. 2, the mother is No. 3, the grandparents Nos. 4-7, and so on. In the English-speaking world its popularity appears to be confined to North America. It is named after Stephan Kekulé von Stradonitz who, in the 1890s, published a book of royal pedigrees using this method. It is also known as the Sosa-Stradonitz method and it is based on the Ahnentafel, developed centuries earlier.

SUPPORT / NETWORKING ORGANISATION

An organisation for people pursuing a career in professional genealogy which offers assistance, puts them in touch with other professionals and even provides them with a platform for promoting their services. A support / networking organisation usually has some type of code of practice, but does not provide any form of accreditation and does not provide any guarantee of competence to clients. Some general membership organisations also fulfil the role of support / networking organisations, for instance in the areas of writing and lecturing.

Bibliography

BOARD FOR CERTIFICATION OF GENEALOGISTS, *The BCG Genealogical Standards Manual* (Washington, DC 2000); rev. edn, as *Genealogy Standards: Fiftieth Anniversary Edition* (Nashville, Tennessee, 2014; Kindle edn, 2014)

CLIFFORD, KAREN, *Becoming an Accredited Genealogist: Plus 100 Tips to Ensure Your Success* (Orem, Utah, 1998)

JACOBUS, DONALD LINUS, *Genealogy as Pastime and Profession* (New Haven, Connecticut, 1930)

JETTÉ, RENÉ, *Traité de généalogie* (Montreal, 1991)

JONES, THOMAS W., *Mastering Genealogical Documentation* (Arlington, Virginia, 2017)

JONES, THOMAS W., *Mastering Genealogical Proof* (Arlington, Virginia, 2013; Kindle edn, 2013)

KYLE, NOELINE, *Citing Historical Sources: a Manual for Family Historians* (St Agnes, South Australia, 2013)

MACDONALD, IAN G., *Referencing for Genealogists* (Stroud, Gloucestershire, 2018)

MERRIMAN, BRENDA DOUGALL, *About Genealogical Standards of Evidence: a guide for genealogists* (Toronto, 1997); rev. edn, *Genealogical Standards of Evidence: a guide for family historians* (Toronto, 2010)

MEYERINK, KORY L., TRISTAN L. TOLMAN & LINDA K. GULBRANDSEN, eds., *Becoming an Excellent Genealogist: Essays on Professional Research Skills* (Salt Lake City, Utah, 2012; Kindle edn, 2012)

MILLS, ELIZABETH SHOWN, *Evidence! Citation & Analysis for the Family Historian* (Baltimore, Maryland, 1997)

MILLS, ELIZABETH SHOWN, *Evidence Explained: Citing History Sources from Artifacts to Cyberspace* (2007; 3rd edn [rev.], Baltimore, Maryland, 2017; Kindle edn, 2015)

MILLS, ELIZABETH SHOWN, ed., *Professional Genealogy: a Manual for Researchers, Writers, Editors, Lecturers and Librarians* (Baltimore, Maryland, 2001) [*ProGen I*]

MILLS, ELIZABETH SHOWN, ed., *Professional Genealogy: Preparation, Practice & Standards* (Baltimore, Maryland, 2018) [*ProGen PPS*]

OXFORD UNIVERSITY PRESS, *New Oxford Style Manual* (3rd edn, Oxford, 2016)

ROSE, CHRISTINE, *Genealogical Proof Standard: Building a Solid Case* (2005; 4th edn, San Jose, California, 2014)

RUBINCAM, MILTON, ed., *Genealogical Research: Methods and Sources* (Washington, DC, 1960)

PHILLIMORE, WPW, *How to Write the History of a Family: A guide for the genealogist* (London, 1888)

SHARPE, MICHAEL, *Family Matters: A history of genealogy* (Barnsley, 2011)

STEVENSON, NOEL C., *Genealogical Evidence: A Guide to the Standard of Proof Relating to Pedigrees, Ancestry, Heirship, and Family History* (1979; rev. edn Laguna Hills, California, 1989)

STRYKER-RODDA, KENN, ed., *Genealogical Research: Methods and Sources*, rev. edn (Washington, DC, 1983)

About the Author

Paul Gorry has been a local and family history enthusiast since childhood and a professional genealogical researcher from the age of nineteen. He has held professional credentials since 1987 from Accredited Genealogists Ireland and has served as the organisation's Hon. Secretary and President. Paul was the originator and chairman of the Irish Genealogical Congress, an international conference on Irish family history worldwide, held in Ireland in 1991, 1994, 1997 and 2001. Due to his interest in local and family history he has been a long-term member of the Co. Kildare Archaeological Society, the West Wicklow Historical Society, the Irish Genealogical Research Society and the Society of Genealogists [London]. He is also a member of the International Society of Family History Writers and Editors. With his AGI colleague Máire Mac Conghail, Paul was joint-author of *Tracing Irish Ancestors* (Glasgow, 1997). He has written three other published books, as well as two privately circulated family histories for clients. Paul is a Fellow of both the Society of Genealogists and the Irish Genealogical Research Society.

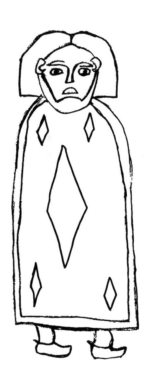

Index

—

Israel
38

Jacobus, Donald Lines
12, 13, 14, 19, 42, 77, 82
Jakman, Alan
34, 129
Johnson, Keith A.
23
Jones, Thomas W.
45, 48, 130, 131

King, Dee Dee
35, 37
Kyle, Noeline
51

LaCount, Louise
18
language
    French   71, 100, 101, 128, 138, 193, 194, 195, 197, 200
    German   32, 39, 87, 128, 200, 207-208
    Polish   33, 129
    Spanish   71, 100, 101, 104, 105, 129, 139, 200
    Swedish   200
Lawson, Leslie Brinkley
35, 36
LDS Church
11, 15, 76, 105
Leary, Helen F.M.
44
Lee, Lisa B.
98, 99
legal genealogy
32, 34, 35, 36, 55, 128, 209
Library of Congress (Washington, DC)
15

Local Historian, The (periodical)
19
Lyon King of Arms, Lord
26, 176

McCabe, John
29
McElroy, David
28
MacLeod, Alan
26
MacRae, Allan
27
Maître généalogiste agréé (see MGA)
Marble, Allan
27
Maritime Premiers, Council of
27
Marshall, George William
10
Marson, Ian
23, 24, 25
Massachusetts Society of Mayflower Descendants
11
Mastering Genealogical Proof (book by Jones)
45
Mathews, Barbara Jean
33, 34, 35
Mexico
199
Meyerink, Kory L.
11, 18, 45
Meyers, Kelvin L.
35
MGA
28, 192, 194